Farnham Bishop

The Story of the Submarine

Farnham Bishop

The Story of the Submarine

ISBN/EAN: 9783955640613

Auflage: 1

Erscheinungsjahr: 2013

Erscheinungsort: Bremen, Deutschland

@ EHV-History in Access Verlag GmbH, Fahrenheitstr. 1, 28359 Bremen. Alle Rechte beim Verlag und bei den jeweiligen Lizenzgebern.

THE STORY OF
THE SUBMARINE

BY
FARNHAM BISHOP
Author of "Panama, Past and Present," etc.

*ILLUSTRATED WITH PHOTOGRAPHS
AND DRAWINGS*

NEW YORK
THE CENTURY CO.
1916

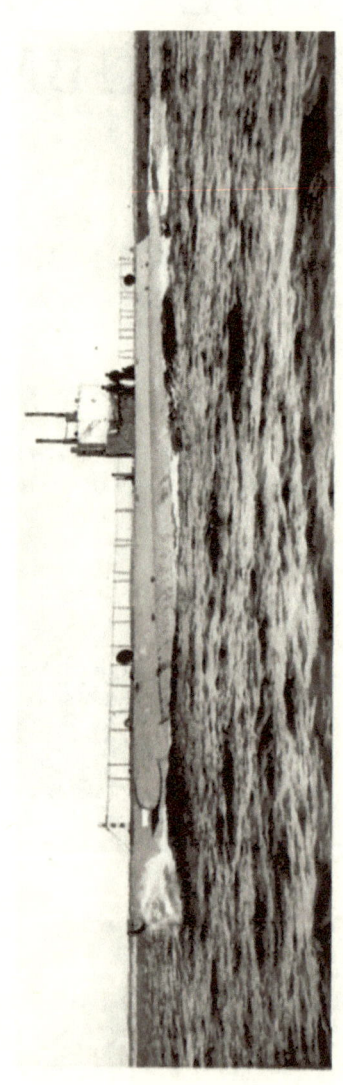

Courtesy of the Electric Boat Company.

U. S. Submarine *M–1*.

PREFACE

This book has been written for the nontechnical reader — for the man or boy who is interested in submarines and torpedoes, and would like to know something about the men who invented these things and how they came to do it. Much has been omitted that I should have liked to have put in, for this is a small book and the story of the submarine is much longer than most people realize. It is perhaps astonishing to think of the launching of an underseaboat in the year the Pilgrims landed at Plymouth Rock, or George Washington watching his submarine attack the British fleet in 1776. But are these things as astonishing as the thought of European soldiers wearing steel helmets and fighting with crossbows and catapults in 1916?

The chapter on " A Trip in a Modern Submarine " is purely imaginative. There is no such boat in our submarine flotilla as the *X-4*. We ought to have plenty of big, fast, sea-going submarines, with plenty of big, fast sea-planes and battle-cruisers, so that if an invading army ever starts for this country we can meet it and smash it while it is cooped up on transports somewhere in mid-ocean. There, and not in shallow, off-shore waters, cumbered with nets and mines, is the true battlefield of the submarine.

The last part of this book has a broken-off and frag-

Preface

mentary appearance. This is almost unavoidable at a time when writing history is like trying to make a statue of a moving-picture. I have tried to do justice to both sides in the present war.

I wish to express my thanks to those whose kindness and courtesy have made it possible for me to write this book. To Mr. Kelby, Librarian of the New York Historical Society, I am indebted for much information about Bushnell's *Turtle,* and to Mrs. Daniel Whitney, of Germantown, Pa., a descendant of Ezra Lee, for the portrait of her intrepid ancestor. Both the Electric Boat Company and Mr. Simon Lake have supplied me most generously with information and pictures. The Bureau of Construction, United States Navy, E. P. Dutton & Company, publishers of Mr. Alan H. Burgoyne's "Submarine Navigation Past and Present"; the American Magazine, Flying, International Marine Engineering, the *Scientific American,* and the *New York Sun* have cheerfully given permission for the reproduction of many pictures of which they hold the copyright. Albert Frank & Company have given the cut of the advertisement of the last sailing of the *Lusitania.* Special thanks are due to Mr. A. Russell Bond, Associate Editor of the *Scientific American,* for expert advice and suggestion.

Some well-known pictures of submarines are herein credited for the first time to the man who made them: Captain Francis M. Barber, U. S. N. (retired). This officer published a little pink-backed pamphlet on submarine boats — the first book devoted exclusively to this subject — in 1875.

"The last time I heard of that pink pamphlet," writes

Preface

Captain Barber from Washington, " was when I was Naval Attache at Berlin in 1898. Admiral von Tirpitz was then head of the Torpedo Bureau in the Navy Department, and he was good enough to say that it was the foundation of his studies — and look what we have now in the terrible German production."

FARNHAM BISHOP.

New York,
   January, 1916.

CONTENTS

CHAPTER		PAGE
I	IN THE BEGINNING	3
II	DAVID BUSHNELL'S "TURTLE"	12
III	ROBERT FULTON'S "NAUTILUS"	26
IV	SUBMARINES IN THE CIVIL WAR	36
V	THE WHITEHEAD TORPEDO	43
VI	FREAKS AND FAILURES	56
VII	JOHN P. HOLLAND	69
VIII	THE LAKE SUBMARINES	82
IX	A TRIP IN A MODERN SUBMARINE	100
X	ACCIDENTS AND SAFETY DEVICES	124
XI	MINES	139
XII	THE SUBMARINE IN ACTION	156
XIII	THE SUBMARINE BLOCKADE	177
XIV	THE SUBMARINE AND NEUTRALS	189
	INDEX	207

List of Illustrations

	PAGE
U. S. Submarine *M–1*	*Frontispiece*
Cornelius Van Drebel	5
The *Rotterdam Boat*	8
Symons's Submarine	10
The Submarine of 1776	13
The Best-known Picture of Bushnell's *Turtle*	16
Another Idea of Bushnell's *Turtle*	19
Ezra Lee	21
The *Nautilus* Invented by Robert Fulton	28
Destruction of the *Dorothea*	33
Views of a Confederate *David*	37
C. S. S. *Hundley*	38
Cross-section of a Whitehead Torpedo	51
Davis Gun-torpedo After Discharge, Showing Eight-inch Gun Forward of Air-flask	53
Effect of Davis Gun-torpedo on a Specially-constructed Target	54
The *Intelligent Whale*	58
Le Plongeur	59
Steam Submarine *Nordenfeldt II*, at Constantinople, 1887	62
Bauer's Submarine Concert, Cronstadt Harbor, 1855	65
Apostoloff's Proposed Submarine	67
The *Holland No. 1*	70

xiv List of Illustrations

	PAGE
The *Fenian Ram*	73
U. S. S. *Holland*, in Drydock with the Russian Battle-ship *Retvizan*	77
John P. Holland	80
Lake 1893 Design as Submitted to the U. S. Navy Department	83
The *Argonaut Junior*	84
Argonaut as Originally Built	87
Argonaut as Rebuilt	90
The Rebuilt *Argonaut,* Showing Pipe-masts and Ship-shaped Superstructure	93
Cross-section of Diving-compartment on a Lake Submarine	94
Cross-section of the *Protector*	97
Mr. Simon Lake	98
U. S. Submarine *E–2*	101
A Submarine Cruiser, or Fleet Submarine (Lake Type)	105
Auxiliary Switchboard and Electric Cook-stove, in a U. S. Submarine	107
Forward Deck of a U. S. Submarine, in Cruising Trim	109
Same, Preparing to Submerge	110
Depth-control Station, U. S. Submarine	113
Cross-section of a Periscope	114
Forward Torpedo-compartment, U. S. Submarine	117
Fessenden Oscillator Outside the Hull of a Ship	120
Professor Fessenden Receiving a Message Sent Through Several Miles of Sea-water by His "Oscillator"	121
Side-elevation of a Modern Submarine	127
One Type of Safety-jacket	131

List of Illustrations

	PAGE
The *Vulcan* Salvaging the *U–3*	134
Fulton's Anchored Torpedoes	140
Sinking of the U. S. S. *Tecumseh*, by a Confederate Mine, in Mobile Bay	143
A Confederate "Keg-torpedo"	144
First Warship Destroyed by a Mine	145
A Confederate "Buoyant Torpedo" or Contact-mine	146
Modern Contact-mine	150
U. S. Mine-planter *San Francisco*	153
English Submarine Rescuing English Sailors	157
Engagement Between the *Birmingham* and the *U–15*	159
Sinking of the *Aboukir*, *Cressy*, and *Hogue*	163
Tiny Target Afforded by Periscopes in Rough Weather	167
Photograph of a Submarine, Twenty Feet Below the Surface, Taken from the Aeroplane, Whose Shadow Is Shown in the Picture	173
German Submarine Pursuing English Merchantman	182
British Submarine, Showing One Type of Disappearing Deck-gun Now in Use	190

THE STORY OF THE SUBMARINE

THE STORY OF THE SUBMARINE

CHAPTER I

IN THE BEGINNING

IF you had been in London in the year 1624, and had gone to the theater to see "The Staple of News," a new and very dull comedy by Shakespeare's friend Ben Jonson, you would have heard, in act III, scene i, the following dialogue about submarines:

THOMAS

They write hear one Cornelius' son
Hath made the Hollanders an invisible eel
To swim the haven at Dunkirk and sink all
The shipping there.

PENNYBOY

But how is 't done?

GRABAL

I'll show you, sir,
It is an automa, runs under water
With a snug nose, and has a nimble tail
Made like an auger, with which tail she wriggles
Betwixt the costs of a ship and sinks it straight.

PENNYBOY

Whence have you this news?

FITTON

From a right hand I assure you.
The eel-boats here, that lie before Queen-hythe
Came out of Holland.

PENNYBOY

A most brave device
To murder their flat bottoms.

The idea of submarine navigation is much older than 1624. Crude diving bells, and primitive leather diving helmets, with bladders to keep the upper end of the air tube afloat on the surface of the water, were used as early as the fourteenth century. William Bourne, an Englishman who published a book on "Inventions or Devices" in 1578, suggested the military value of a boat that could be sailed just below the surface of the water, with a hollow mast for a ventilator. John Napier, Laird of Merchiston, the great Scotch mathematician who invented logarithms, wrote in 1596 about his proposed "Devices of sailing under the water, with divers other devices and stratagems for the burning of enemies."

But the first man actually to build and navigate a submarine was a Dutchman: the learned Doctor Cornelius Van Drebel.[1] He was "a native of Alkmaar, a very fair and handsome man, and of very gentle manners." Both his pleasing personality and his knowledge of sci-

---

[1] Also spelled Van Drebbel, Drebell, Dreble, and Trebel. He is the man Ben Jonson calls "Cornelius' son."

ence — which caused many to suspect him of being a magician — made the Netherlander an honored guest at the court of his most pedantic Majesty, King James I of England.

Van Drebel was walking along the banks of the Thames, one pleasant evening in the year 1620, when he "noticed some sailors dragging behind their barques baskets full of fish; he saw that the barques were weighed down in the water, but that they rose a little when the baskets allowed the ropes which held them to slacken a little. The idea occurred to him that a ship could be held under water by a somewhat similar method and could be propelled by oars and poles."[2]

Cornelius Van Drebel.

Reproduced from "Submarine Navigation, Past and Present" by Alan H. Burgoyne, by permission of E. P. Dutton & Company.

Lodged by the king in Eltham Palace, and supplied with funds from the royal treasury, Van Drebel designed and built three submarine boats, between 1620 and 1624.

[2] Harsdoffer.

They were simply large wooden rowboats, decked over and made water-tight by a covering of thick, well-greased leather. Harsdoffer, a chronicler of the period, declared that

"King James himself journeyed in one of them on the Thames. There were on this occasion twelve rowers besides the passengers, and the vessel during several hours was kept at a depth of twelve to fifteen feet below the surface."

Another contemporary historian, Cornelius Van der Wonde, of Van Drebel's home town, said of him:

"He built a ship in which one could row and navigate under water from Westminster to Greenwich, the distance of two Dutch miles; even five or six miles or as far as one pleased. In this boat a person could see under the surface of the water and without candle-light, as much as he needed to read in the Bible or any other book. Not long ago this remarkable ship was yet to be seen lying in the Thames or London river."

The glow of phosphorescent bodies, suggested by the monk Mersenne for illuminating the interior of a submarine, later in the seventeenth century and actually so used by Bushnell in the eighteenth, might have furnished sufficient light for Bible- and compass-reading on this voyage. But how did King James — the first and last monarch to venture on an underwater voyage — the other passengers, and the twelve rowers get enough air?

"That deservedly Famous Mechanician and Chymist, Cornelius Drebell . . . conceived, that 't is not only the whole body of the air but a certain Quintessence (as Chymists speake) or spirituous part that makes it fit for

In the Beginning

respiration . . . so that (for aught I could gather) besides the Mechanicall contrivance of his vessel he had a Chymicall liquor, which he accounted the chief secret of his Submarine Navigation. For when from time to time he perceived that the finer and purer part of the air was consumed or over-clogged by the respiration and steames of those that went in his ship, he would, by unstopping a vessel full of liquor speedily restore to the troubled air such a proportion of vital parts as would make it again for a good while fit for Respiration." [3]

Did Van Drebel anticipate by one hundred and fifty years the discovery of oxygen: the life-giving "Quintessence" of air? Even if he did, it is incredible that he should have found a liquid, utterly unknown to modern chemistry, capable of giving off that gas so freely that a few gallons would restore the oxygen to a confined body of air as fast as fifteen or twenty men could consume it by breathing. Perhaps his "Chymicall liquor" instead of producing oxygen directly, increased the proportion of it in the atmosphere by absorbing the carbonic acid gas.

The Abbé de Hautefeullie, who wrote in 1680 on "Methods of breathing under water," made the following shrewd guess at the nature of the apparatus:

"Drebel's secret was probably the machine which I had imagined, consisting of a bellows with two valves and two tubes resting on the surface of the water, the one bringing down air and the other sending it back. By speaking of a volatile essence which restored the nitrous

---

[3] "New Experiments touching the Spring of the Air and its Effects," by Robert Boyle, Oxford, 1662, p. 188.

parts consumed by respiration, Drebel evidently wished to disguise his invention and prevent others from finding out its real nature."

It is a very great pity that we know no more about these earliest submarines. Cornelius Van Drebel died in 1634, at the age of sixty-two, without leaving any written notes or oral descriptions. We must not think too hardly of this inventor of three centuries ago, unguarded by patent laws, for making a mystery of his

Courtesy of the Scientific American.

The *Rotterdam Boat*.

discoveries. He had to be a showman as well as a scientist, or his noble patrons would have lost all interest in his "ingenious machines," and mystery is half of the showman's game. Besides his "eel-boats," Van Drebel is said to have invented a wonderful globe with which he imitated perpetual motion and illustrated the course of the sun, moon, and stars; an incubator, a refrigerator, "Virginals that played of themselves," and other marvels too numerous to mention. Half scientist, half charlatan,

In the Beginning

wholly medieval in appearance, with his long furred gown and long, fair beard, Cornelius Van Drebel marches picturesquely at the head of the procession of inventors who have made possible the modern submarine.

Eighteen years after Van Drebel's death, a Frenchman named Le Son built a submarine at Rotterdam. This craft, which is usually referred to as the *Rotterdam Boat,* was 72 feet long, 12 feet high, and of 8 foot beam. It was built of wood, with sharply tapering ends, and had a superstructure whose sloping sides were designed to deflect cannon balls that might be fired at the boat while traveling on the surface, while iron-shod legs protected the hull when resting on the sea bottom. A single paddlewheel amidships was to propel the boat,— just how, the inventor never revealed. Like so many other submarines, the *Rotterdam Boat* was built primarily to be used against the British fleet. But it failed to interest either the Dutch or French minister of marine, and never went into action.

The earliest known contemporary picture of a submarine vessel appeared in the "Gentleman's Magazine," in 1747. It showed a cross section of an underwater boat built and navigated on the Thames by one Symons. This was a decked-over row-boat, propelled by four pairs of oars working in water-tight joints of greased leather. To submerge his vessel, Symons admitted water into a number of large leather bottles, placed inside the hull with their open mouth passing through holes in the bottom. When he wished to rise, he would squeeze out the water with a lever and bind up the neck of each emptied bottle with string. This ingenious device was not original with Mr. Symons, but was invented by a Frenchman named Borelli in 1680.

Submarine navigation was a century and a half old before it claimed its first victim. J. Day, an English mechanic, rebuilt a small boat so that he was able to submerge it in thirty feet of water, with himself on board, and remain there for twenty-four hours with no ill effect. At the end of this time, Day rose to the surface, absolutely certain of his ability to repeat the ex-

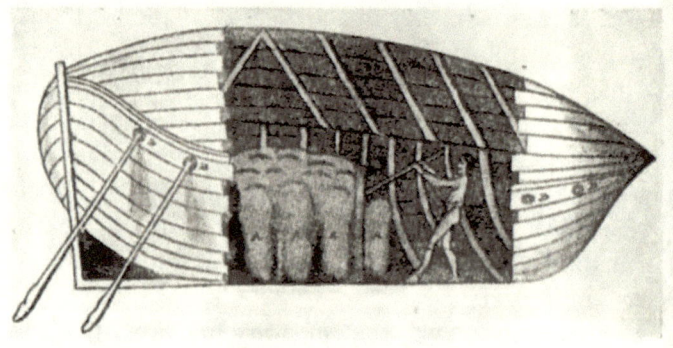

Symons's Submarine.

periment at any depth. But how could he turn this to practical account?

It was an age of betting, when gentlemen could always be found to risk money on any wager, however fantastic. Day found a financial backer in a Mr. Blake, who advanced him the money to buy a fifty-ton sloop and fit it with a strong water-tight compartment amidships. Ten tons of ballast were placed in the hold and twenty more hung outside the hull by four iron rods passing through the passenger's compartment. When the rest

In the Beginning

of the boat was filled with water, it would sink to the bottom, to rise again when the man inside released the twenty tons of outer ballast.

Shut in the water-tight compartment of this boat, Day sank to the bottom of Plymouth Harbor, at 2 P.M., Tuesday, June 28, 1774, to decide a bet that he could remain twelve hours at a depth of twenty-two fathoms (132 feet). When, at the expiration of this time, the submarine failed to reappear, Mr. Blake called on the captain of a near-by frigate for help. Bluejackets from the warship and workmen from the dockyard were set to work immediately to grapple for the sunken craft and raise her to the surface, but to no avail. The great pressure of water at that depth — 150 feet is the limit of safety for many modern submarines — must have crushed in the walls of the water-tight compartment without giving Day time enough to release the outer ballast and rise to safety.

CHAPTER II

DAVID BUSHNELL'S "TURTLE"

IN the first week of September, 1776, the American army defending New York still held Manhattan Island, but nothing more. Hastily improvised, badly equipped, and worse disciplined, it had been easily defeated by a superior invading force of British regulars and German mercenaries in the battle of Long Island. Brooklyn had fallen; from Montauk Point to the East River, all was the enemy's country. Staten Island, too, was an armed and hostile land. After the fall of the forts on both sides of the Narrows, the British fleet had entered the Upper Bay, and even landed marines and infantry on Governor's Island. Grimly guarding the crowded transports, the ship-of-the-line *Asia* and the frigate *Eagle* lay a little above Staten Island, with their broadsides trained on the doomed city.

In the mouth of the North River, not a biscuit-toss from the Battery, floated the brass conning-tower of an American submarine.

It was the only submarine in the world and its inventor called it the *Turtle*. He called it that because it looked like one: a turtle floating with its tail down and a conning-tower for a head. It has also been compared to a modern soldier's canteen with an extra-large mouthpiece, or a hardshell clam wearing a silk hat. It was

David Bushnell's "Turtle"

deeper than it was long and not much longer than it was broad. It had no periscope, torpedo tubes, or cage of white mice. But the *Turtle* was a submarine, for all that.

Its inventor was a Connecticut Yankee, Mr. David Bushnell, later Captain Bushnell of the corps of sappers and miners and in the opinion of his Excellency General Washington "a man of great mechanical powers, fertile in invention and master of execution." Bushnell was born in Saybrook and educated at Yale, where he graduated with the class of 1775. During his four years as an undergraduate, he spent most of his spare time solving the problem of exploding gunpowder under water.

The Submarine of 1776.
(As described by its operator.)

A water-tight case would keep his powder dry, but how could he get a spark inside to explode it? Percussion caps had not yet been invented, but Bushnell took the flintlock from a musket and had it snapped by clockwork that could be wound up and set for any desired length of time.

"The first experiment I made," wrote Bushnell in a letter to Thomas Jefferson when the latter was American minister to France in 1789, "was with about 2 ounces of powder, which I exploded 4 feet under water, to prove to some of the first personages in Connecticut that powder would take fire under water.

"The second experiment was made with 2 lb. of powder enclosed in a wooden bottle and fixed under a hogshead, with a 2-inch oak plank between the hogshead and the powder. The hogshead was loaded with stones as deep as it could swim; a wooden pipe, descending through the lower head of the hogshead and through the plank into the bottle, was primed with powder. A match put to the priming exploded the powder, which produced a very great effect, rending the plank into pieces, demolishing the hogshead, and casting the stones and the ruins of the hogshead, with a body of water, many feet into the air, to the astonishment of the spectators. This experiment was likewise made for the satisfaction of the gentlemen above mentioned."

Governor Trumbull of Connecticut was among the "first personages" present at these experiments, which so impressed him and his council that they appropriated enough money for Bushnell to build the *Turtle*. The Nutmeg State was thus the first "world-power" to have a submarine in its navy.[1]

The hull of the *Turtle* was not made of copper, as is sometimes stated, but was "built of oak, in the strongest

---

[1] The only submarine built before this for military purposes, the *Rotterdam Boat*, remained private property, and King James's "eelboats" were merely pleasure craft.

David Bushnell's "Turtle"

manner possible, corked and tarred."[2] The conning-tower was of brass and also served as a hatch-cover. The hatchway was barely big enough for the one man who made up the entire crew to squeeze through. Once inside, the operator could screw the cover down tight, and look out through "three round doors, one directly in front and one on each side, large enough to put the hand through. When open they admitted fresh air." On top of the conning-tower were two air-pipes "so constructed that they shut themselves whenever the water rose near their tops, so that no water could enter through them and opened themselves immediately after they rose above the water.

"The vessel was chiefly ballasted with lead fixed to its bottom; when this was not sufficient a quantity was placed within, more or less according to the weight of the operator; its ballast made it so stiff that there was no danger of oversetting. The vessel, with all its appendages and the operator, was of sufficient weight to settle it very low in the water. About 200 lb. of lead at the bottom for ballast could be let down 40 or 50 feet below the vessel; this enabled the operator to rise instantly to the surface of the water in case of accident."

The operator sat on an oaken brace that kept the two sides of the boat from being crushed in by the water-pressure, and did things with his hands and feet. He must have been as busy as a cathedral organist on Easter morning. With one foot he opened a brass valve that let

[2] Sergeant Ezra Lee's letter to Gen. David Humphreys, written in 1815. Published in the "Magazine of American History," Vol. 29, p. 261.

water into the ballast tanks, with the other he worked a force pump to drive it out. When he had reached an approximate equilibrium, he could move the submarine up or down, or hold it at any desired depth, by cranking a small vertical-acting propellor placed just forward of the conning-tower on the deck above. Before him was the crank of another propellor, or rather tractor, for it drew, not pushed, the vessel forward. Behind him was the rudder, which the operator controlled with a long curved tiller stuck under one arm.

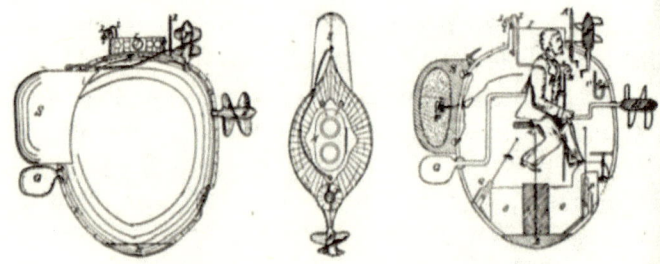

The Best-known Picture of Bushnell's *Turtle*.
Drawn by Lieutenant F. M. Barber, U. S. N., in 1875.

Bushnell, in his letter to Jefferson, calls each of these propellors "an oar, formed upon the principle of the screw," and the best-known picture of the *Turtle* shows a bearded gentleman in nineteenth-century clothes boring his way through the water with two big gimlets. But Sergeant Ezra Lee of the Connecticut Line, who did the actual operating, described the submarine's forward propellor (he makes no mention of the other) as having two wooden blades or "oars, of about 12 inches in length and 4 or 5 in width, shaped like the arms of a windmill."

Except in size, this device must have looked very much like the wooden-bladed tractor of a modern aeroplane.

"These oars," noted Judge Griswold on the letter before forwarding it to General Humphrey, "were fixed on the end of a shaft like windmill arms projected out forward, and turned at right angles with the course of the machine; and upon the same principles that wind-mill arms are turned by the wind, these oars, when put in motion as the writer describes, draw the machine slowly after it. This moving power is small, and every attendant circumstance must coöperate with it to answer the purpose — calm waters and no current."

"With hard labor," said Lee, "the machine might be impelled at the rate of '3 nots' an hour for a short time."

Sergeant Lee volunteered "to learn the ways and mystery of this new machine" because the original operator, Bushnell's brother, "was taken sick in the campaign of 1776 at New York before he had an opportunity to make use of his skill, and never recovered his health sufficiently afterwards." While Lee was still struggling with the "mystery" in practice trips on Long Island Sound, the British fleet entered New York Harbor. The submarine was at once hurried to New Rochelle, carted overland to the Hudson, and towed down to the city.

At slack tide on the first calm night after his arrival, Lee screwed down the conning-tower of the *Turtle* above his head and set out to attack the British fleet.[4] Two

---
[4] "General Washington and his associates in the secret took their stations upon a house in Broadway, anxiously awaiting the result."

whaleboats towed him as near as they dared and then cast off. Running awash, with not more than six or seven inches of the conning-tower exposed, the submarine crept, silent and unseen, down the bay and up under the towering stern of his Britannic Majesty's 64-gun frigate *Eagle*.

"When I rowed under the stern of the ship," wrote Sergeant Lee in after years, "I could see the men on deck and hear them talk. I then shut down all the doors, sunk down and came under the bottom of the ship."

Up through the top of the submarine ran a long sharp gimlet, not for boring a hole through the bottom of a ship, but to be screwed into the wooden hull and left there, to serve as an anchor for a mine. Tied to the screw and carried on the after-deck of the *Turtle* was an egg-shaped "magazine," made of two hollowed-out pieces of oak and containing one hundred and fifty pounds of gunpowder, with a clockwork time-fuse that would begin to run as soon as the operator cast off the magazine after making fast the screw. Everything seemed ready for Sergeant Lee to anticipate Lieutenant Commander Von Weddigen by one hundred and thirty-eight years.

But no matter how hard the strong-wristed sergeant turned the handle, he could not drive the screw into the frigate's hull. The *Eagle* was copper-sheathed![5]

"I pulled along to try another place," said Lee, "but deviated a little to one side and immediately rose with

From Ezra Lee's obituary, New York "Commercial Advertiser," November 15, 1821.

[5] According to Bushnell, the screw struck an iron bar securing the rudder.

David Bushnell's "Turtle"

great velocity and came above the surface 2 or 3 feet, between the ship and the daylight, then sunk again like a porpoise. I hove about to try again, but on further thought I gave out, knowing that as soon as it was light the ships' boats would be rowing in all directions, and I thought the best generalship was to retreat as fast as I could, as I had 4 miles to go before passing Governor's Island. So I jogg'd on as fast as I could."

To enable him to steer a course when submerged, Lee

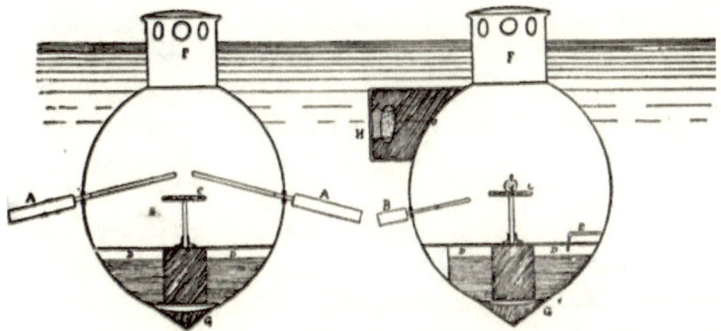

Another Idea of Bushnell's *Turtle*.

had before him a compass, most ingeniously illuminated with phosphorescent pieces of rotten wood. But for some reason this proved to be of no use.

"I was obliged to rise up every few minutes to see that I sailed in the right direction, and for this purpose keeping the machine on the surface of the water and the doors open. I was much afraid of getting aground on the island, as the tide of the flood set on the north point.

"While on my passage up to the city, my course, owing to the above circumstances, was very crooked and zigzag, and the enemy's attention was drawn towards me from Governor's Island. When I was abreast of the fort on the island, 3 or 400 men got upon the parapet to observe me; at length a number came down to the shore, shoved off a 12 oar'd barge with 5 or 6 sitters and pulled for me. I eyed them, and when they had got within 50 or 60 yards of me I let loose the magazine in hopes that if they should take me they would likewise pick up the magazine, and then we should all be blown up together. But as kind Providence would have it, they took fright and returned to the island to my infinite joy. I then weathered the island, and our people seeing me, came off with a whaleboat and towed me in. The magazine, after getting a little past the island, went off with a tremendous explosion, throwing up large bodies of water to an immense height."

A few days afterwards, the British forces landed on Manhattan Island at what is now the foot of East Thirty-fourth Street, and Washington's army hastily withdrew to the Harlem Heights, above One Hundred and Twenty-fifth Street. A British frigate sailed up the Hudson and anchored off Bloomingdale, or between Seventy-second and One Hundred and Tenth Streets, in the same waters where our Atlantic fleet lies whenever it comes to town. Here Sergeant Lee in the *Turtle* made two more attempts. But the first time he was discovered by the watch, and when he approached again, submerged, the phosphorus-painted cork that served as an indicator in his crude but ingenious depth-gage, got caught and deceived him so that he dived completely under the warship without touching her. Shortly after this, the frigate came up the river,

Ezra Lee.
Born at Lyme, Conn., Jan. 21, 1749,
Died at Lyme, Conn., Oct. 29, 1821.

From original painting in possession of his descendant, Mrs. Daniel Whitney, 5117 Pulaski Avenue, Germantown, Pa.

overhauled the sloop on which the *Turtle* was being transported, and sent it to the bottom, submarine and all.

"Though I afterwards recovered the vessel," Bushnell wrote to Jefferson, "I found it impossible at that time to prosecute the design any further. I had been in a bad state of health from the beginning of my undertaking, and was now very unwell; the situation of public affairs was such that I despaired of obtaining the public attention and the assistance necessary. I was unable to support myself and the persons I must have employed had I proceeded. Besides, I found it absolutely necessary that the operators should acquire more skill in the management of the vessel before I could expect success, which would have taken up some time, and no small additional expense. I therefore gave over the pursuit for that time and waited for a more favorable opportunity, which never arrived.

"In the year 1777 I made an attempt from a whaleboat against the *Cerberus* frigate, then lying at anchor between Connecticut River and New London, by drawing a machine against her side by means of a line. The machine was loaded with powder, to be exploded by a gunlock, which was to be unpinioned by an apparatus to be turned by being brought alongside of the frigate. This machine fell in with a schooner at anchor astern of the frigate, and concealed from my sight. By some means or other it was fired, and demolished the schooner and three men, and blew the only one left alive overboard, who was taken up very much hurt.[6]

[6] This survivor was examined by the captain of the *Cerberus*, who

David Bushnell's "Turtle"

"After this I fixed several kegs under water, charged with powder, to explode upon touching anything as they floated along with the tide. I set them afloat in the Delaware, above the English shipping at Philadelphia, in December, 1777. I was unacquainted with the river, and obliged to depend upon a gentleman very imperfectly acquainted with that part of it, as I afterwards found. We went as near the shipping as we durst venture; I believe the darkness of the night greatly deceived him, as it did me. We set them adrift to fall with the ebb upon the shipping. Had we been within sixty rods I believe they must have fallen in with them immediately, as I designed; but, as I afterwards found, they were set adrift much too far distant, and did not arrive until, after being detained some time by frost, they advanced in the daytime in a dispersed situation and under great disadvantages. One of them blew up a boat with several persons in it who imprudently handled it too freely, and thus gave the British the alarm which brought on the battle of the kegs."

The agitated redcoats lined the banks and blazed away at every bit of drifting wreckage in the river, as described by a sarcastic Revolutionary poet in "The Battle of the Kegs."

> Gallants attend, and hear a friend
> Troll forth harmonious ditty,
> Strange things I'll tell that once befell
> In Philadelphia city.

reported that the schooner's crew had drawn the machine on board and by rashly tampering with its mechanism caused it to explode.

The Story of the Submarine

'Twas early day, as poets say,
Just as the sun was rising,
A soldier stood on a log of wood
And saw a thing surprising.

As in amaze he stood to gaze,
The truth can't be denied, sir,
He spied a score of kegs or more
Come floating down the tide, sir.

. . . .

These kegs, I'm told, the rebels hold
Packed up like pickled herring,
And they're coming down to attack the town,
In this new way of ferrying.

. . . .

Therefore prepare for bloody war,
The kegs must all be routed,
Or surely we despised shall be
And British valor doubted.

The royal band now ready stand
All ranged in dread array, sir,
With stomach stout to see it out
And make a bloody day, sir.

The cannon roar from shore to shore,
The small arms make a rattle,
Since wars began, I'm sure no man
E'er saw so strange a battle.

The kegs, 't is said, though strongly made,
Of rebel staves and hoops, sir,
Could not oppose their powerful foes,
The conquering British troops, sir.

David Bushnell was later captured by the British, who failed to recognize him and soon released him as a harmless civilian. After the Revolution he went to France, and then to Georgia, where disgusted with the Government's neglect of himself and his invention he changed his name to "Dr. Bush." He was eighty-four years old when he died in 1826. His identity was then revealed in his will.

Bushnell found the submarine boat a useless plaything and made it a formidable weapon. To him it owes the propellor, the conning-tower, and the first suggestion of the torpedo. The *Turtle* was not only the first American submarine but the forerunner of the undersea destroyer of to-day.

"I thought and still think that it was an effort of genius," declared George Washington to Thomas Jefferson, "but that too many things were necessary to be combined to expect much against an enemy who are always on guard."

CHAPTER III

ROBERT FULTON'S "NAUTILUS"

ROBERT FULTON was probably the first American who ever went to Paris for the purpose of selling war-supplies to the French government. Unlike his compatriots of to-day, he found anything but a ready market. For three years, beginning in 1797, Fulton tried constantly but vainly to interest the Directory in his plans for a submarine. Though a commission appointed to examine his designs reported favorably, the minister of marine would have nothing to do with them. Fulton built a beautiful little model submarine of mahogany and exhibited it, but with no results. He made an equally fruitless attempt to sell his invention to Holland, then called the Batavian Republic. Nobody seemed to have the slightest belief or interest in submarines.

But Fulton was a persistent man or he would never have got his name into the history books. He stayed in Paris, where his friend Joel Barlow was American minister, and supported himself by inventing and exhibiting what he called "the pictures": the first moving pictures the world had ever seen. These were panoramas, where the picture was not thrown on the screen by a lantern but painted on it, and the long roll of painted canvas was unrolled like a film between two large spools on opposite

Robert Fulton's "Nautilus"

sides of the stage. Very few people remember that Robert Fulton invented the panorama, though only a generation ago the great panorama of the battle of Gettysburg drew and thrilled as large audiences as a film like "The Birth of a Nation" does to-day. Fulton painted his own panoramas himself, for he was an artist before he was an engineer. He made three of them and had to build a separate little theater to show each one in. The Parisians were so well pleased with this novelty that they made up a song about the panoramas, and the street where the most popular of the three was shown is still called "La Rue Fulton." The picture that won the inventor this honor was a panorama of the burning of Moscow — not the burning of the city to drive out Napoleon, for that came a dozen years later, but an earlier conflagration, some time in the eighteenth century.

Napoleon overthrew the Directory and became First Consul and absolute ruler of France in 1800. He appointed three expert naval engineers to examine Fulton's plans, and on their approval, Napoleon advanced him 10,000 francs to build a submarine.

Construction was begun at once and the boat was finished in May, 1801. She was a remarkably modern-looking craft, and a great improvement on everything that had gone before. She was the first submarine to have a fish-shaped, metal hull. It was built of copper plating on iron ribs, and was 21 feet 3 inches long and 6 feet 5 inches in diameter at the thickest point, which was well forward. A heavy keel gave stability and immediately above it were the water-ballast tanks for submerging the vessel. Two men propelled the boat when

28   The Story of the Submarine

beneath the surface by turning a hand-winch geared to the shaft of a two-bladed, metal propellor. (Fulton called the propellor a " fly," and got the idea of it from the little windmill-shaped device placed in the throat of an old-fashioned fireplace to be revolved by the hot air passing up the chimney and used to turn the roasting-

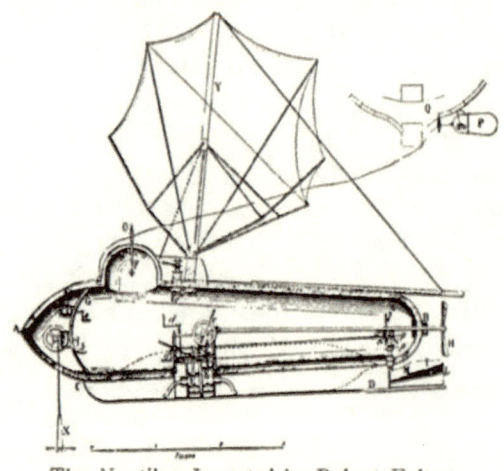

The *Nautilus,* Invented by Robert Fulton.
A-B, Hull; C-D, Keel; E-E, Pumps; F, Conning Tower; G, Bulkhead; H, Propellor; I, Vertical Rudder; L, Horizontal Rudder (diving-plane); M, Pivot attaching horizontal to vertical rudder; N, Gear controlling horizontal rudder; O, " Horn of the *Nautilus;* " P, Torpedo; Q, Hull of vessel attacked; X, Anchor; Y, Mast and sail for use on surface.

spit in many a French kitchen for centuries past.) The third member of the crew stood in the dome-shaped conning-tower and steered, while Fulton himself controlled the pumps, valves, and the diving-planes or horizontal rudders that steered the submarine up and down. Instead of forcing his boat under with a vertical-acting screw, like Bushnell and Nordenfelt (see pages 16 and 62),

Fulton, like Holland, made her dive bow-foremost by depressing her nose with the diving-planes and shoving her under by driving her ahead. Fulton was also the first to give a submarine separate means of propulsion for above and below the surface. Just as a modern undersea boat uses oil-engines whenever it can and saves its storage batteries for use when submerged, Fulton spared the strength of his screw by rigging the *Nautilus* with a mast and sail. By pulling a rope from inside the vessel, the sail could be shut up like a fan, and the hinged mast lowered and stowed away in a groove on deck. Later a jib was added to the mainsail, and the two combined gave the *Nautilus* a surface speed of two knots an hour. She is the only submarine on record that could go faster below the water than above it, for her two-man-power propellor bettered this by half a knot.

Her method of attack was the same as the *Turtle's*. Up through the top of the conning-tower projected what Fulton called the "Horn of the Nautilus." This was an eyeleted spike, to be driven into the bottom of a hostile ship and left there. From a windlass carried in a watertight forward compartment of the submarine, a thin, strong tow-rope ran through the eyehole in the spike to the trigger of a flintlock inside a copper case nearly full of gunpowder, which was not carried on deck, as on the *Turtle*, but towed some distance astern. As soon as this powder-case came to a full stop against the spike, the tow-rope would pull the trigger.

Robert Fulton felt the lack of a distinctive name for such an under-water charge of explosives, till he thought of its likeness to the electric ray, that storage battery of a fish that gives a most unpleasant shock to any one touching it. So he took the first half of this creature's scientific name: *Torpedo electricus*. Fulton had a knack for picking good names. He called his submarine the *Nautilus* because it had a sail which it opened and folded away even as the beautiful shellfish of that name was supposed to furl and unfurl its large, sail-like membrane.

On her first trial on the Seine at Paris, in May, 1801, the *Nautilus* remained submerged for twenty minutes with Fulton and one other man on board, and a lighted candle for them to navigate by. This consumed too much air, however, so a small glass window was placed in the conning-tower, and gave light enough instead. Four men were then able to remain under for an hour. After that, Fulton made the first compressed-air tank, a copper globe containing a cubic foot of compressed air, by drawing on which the submarine's crew could stay under for six hours. This was in the harbor of Brest, where the *Nautilus* had been taken overland. A trial attack was made on an old bulk, which was successfully blown up. The submarine also proved its ability either to furl its sails and dive quickly out of sight, or to cruise for a considerable distance on the surface. Once it sailed for seventy miles down the English Channel.

Fulton had planned a submarine campaign for scaring the British navy and merchant marine out of the narrow seas and so bringing Great Britain to her knees, more than a century before the German emperor proclaimed his famous "war zone" around the British Isles. In one of his letters to the Directory, the American inventor declared that:

"The enormous commerce of England, no less than its monstrous Government, depends upon its military marine. Should some vessels of war be destroyed by means so novel, so hidden, and so incalculable, the confidence of the seamen will vanish and the fleet will be rendered useless from the moment of the first terror."

To a friend in America, Fulton wrote from Paris on November 20, 1798:

"I would ask any one if all the American difficulties during this war are not owing to the naval systems of Europe and a licensed robbery on the ocean? How then is America to prevent this? Certainly not by attempting to build a fleet to cope with the fleets of Europe, but if possible by rendering the European fleets useless."

Fulton began his campaign by an attack on two brigs, the nearest vessels of the English blockading fleet. But whenever the *Nautilus* left port for this purpose, both brigs promptly stood out to sea and remained there till the submarine went home. Unknown to Fulton, his actions were being closely watched by the English secret service, whose spies were always able to send a timely warning to the British fleet. During the day time, when the *Nautilus* was about, the warships were kept under full sail, with lookouts in the crosstrees watching with telescopes for the first glimpse of its sail or conning-tower. At night, the frigates and ships-of-the-line were guarded by picket-boats rowing round and round them, just as modern dreadnoughts are guarded by destroyers.

Disappointed by the lack of results, the French naval authorities refused either to let Fulton build a larger and more efficient submarine, or to grant commissions in the navy to him and his crew. He wanted some assurance that in case they were captured they would not be hanged by the British, who then as now denounced submarine warfare by others as little better than piracy. To guarantee their own safety, Fulton proposed that the French government threaten to retaliate by hanging an equal number of English prisoners, but it was pointed out to him that this would only lead to further executions by the British, who had many more French prisoners of war than there were captive Englishmen in France.

Napoleon had lost faith in the submarine, nor could Fulton interest him in a steamboat which he now built and operated on the Seine, till it was sunk by the weight of the machinery breaking the hull in two. So Fulton quit France and crossed over to England, where Mr. Pitt, the prime minister, was very much interested in his inventions.

Fulton succeeded in planting one of his torpedoes under an old empty Danish brig, the *Dorothea*, in Deal Harbor, in front of Walmer Castle, Pitt's own residence, on October 15, 1805. The prime minister had had to hurry back to London, but there were many naval officers present, and one of them declared loudly that he would be quite unconcerned if he were sitting at dinner at that moment in the cabin of the *Dorothea*. Ten minutes later the clockwork ran out and the torpedo exploded, breaking the brig in two amidships and hurling the fragments high in the air. The success of this experiment was not entirely pleasing to the heads of the British navy. Their opinion was voiced by Admiral Lord St. Vincent, who declared that:

Robert Fulton's "Nautilus"

"Pitt was the greatest fool that ever existed, to encourage a mode of war which they who command the seas did not want and which if successful would deprive them of it."

Six days after the destruction of the *Dorothea*, the sea-

Destruction of the *Dorothea*.
From a woodcut by Robert Fulton.

power of France was broken by Nelson at the battle of Trafalgar. Napoleon now gave up all hope of gaining the few hours' control of the Channel that would have enabled him to invade England, and broke up the camp of his Grand Army that had waited so long at

Boulogne. With this danger gone, England was no longer interested in submarines and torpedoes. So Fulton returned to America, to build the *Clairmont* and win his place in history. But to him, steam navigation was far less important than submarine warfare. In the letter to his old friend Joel Barlow, dated New York, August 22, 1807, in which he described the first voyage of the *Clairmont* up the Hudson, Fulton said:

"However, I will not admit that it is half so important as the torpedo system of defense or attack, for out of this will grow the liberty of the seas — an object of infinite importance to the welfare of America and every civilized country. But thousands of witnesses have now seen the steamboat in rapid movement and they believe; but they have not seen a ship of war destroyed by a torpedo, and they do not believe. We cannot expect people in general to have knowledge of physics or power to reason from cause to effect, but in case we have war and the enemy's ships come into our waters, if the government will give me reasonable means of action, I will soon convince the world that we have surer and cheaper modes of defense than they are aware of."

Fulton had been having his troubles with the navy department. Soon after his return to this country he had made his usual demonstration of torpedoing a small anchored vessel, but it was not until 1810 that he was given the opportunity to make a test attack on a United States warship. But stout old Commodore Rogers, who had been entrusted with the defense of the brig *Argus,* under which Fulton was to plant a torpedo, anchored the vessel in shallow water, stretched a tight wall of spars and netting all round her, and successfully defied the inventor to blow her up. Even a modern destroyer or submarine would be puzzled to get past this defense. Though compelled to admit his failure, Fulton pointed out that "a system then in its infancy, which compelled a hostile vessel to guard herself by such extraordinary means, could not fail of becoming a most important mode of warfare."

It was a great triumph for conservatism — the same spirit of conservatism that threatens to send our navy into its next war with no battle-cruisers, too few scouts and sea-planes, and the slowest dreadnoughts in the world. Though Fulton published a wonderful little book on "Torpedo War and Submarine Explosions" in New York in 1810, the United States navy made no use of it in the War of 1812. A privateer submarine from Connecticut made three dives under the British battleship *Ramillies* off New London, but failed to attach a torpedo for the old reason: copper sheathing. Further attacks were prevented by the captain of the *Ramillies,* who gave notice that he had had a number of American prisoners placed on board as hostages. Fulton himself was hard at work superintending the building both of the *Demologos,* the first steam-propelled battleship, and the *Mute,* a large armored submarine that was to carry a silent engine and a crew of eighty men, when he died in 1815.

CHAPTER IV

SUBMARINES IN THE CIVIL WAR

THE most powerful battleship in the world, half a century ago, was the U.S.S. *New Ironsides*. She was a wooden-hulled, ship-rigged steamer of 3486 tons displacement — about one tenth the size of a modern superdreadnought — her sides plated with four inches of iron armor, and carrying twenty heavy guns. On the night of October 5, 1863, the *New Ironsides* was on blockade duty off Charleston Harbor, when Ensign Howard, the officer of the deck, saw something approaching that looked like a floating plank. He hailed it, and was answered by a rifle ball that stretched him, mortally wounded, on the deck. An instant later came the flash and roar of a tremendous explosion, a column of water shot high into the air alongside, and the *New Ironsides* was shaken violently from stem to stern.

The Confederate submarine *David* had crept up and driven a spar-torpedo against Goliath's armor.

But except for a few splintered timbers, a flooded engine-room, and a marine's broken leg, no damage had been done. As the Confederate craft was too close and too low in the water for the broadside guns to bear, the crew of the ironclad lined the rail and poured volley after volley of musketry into their dimly seen adversary till she drifted away into the night. Her crew of seven men had dived overboard at the moment of impact, and were all picked up by different vessels of the blockading fleet, except the engineer and one other, who swam back to the *David,* started her engine again, and brought her safely home to Charleston.

The *David* was a cigar-shaped steam launch, fifty-four feet long and six feet broad at the thickest point. Pro-

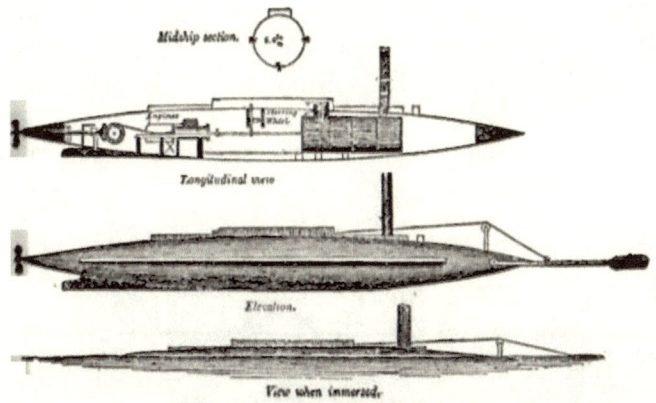

Views of a Confederate *David.*
From Scharf's History of the Confederate States Navy.

jecting from her bow was a fifteen-foot spar, with a torpedo charged with sixty pounds of gunpowder at the end of it. This was exploded by the heat given off by certain chemicals, after they were shaken up together by the impact of the torpedo against the enemy's ship. The *David,* steaming at her full speed of seven knots an hour, struck squarely against the *New Ironsides* at the water-line and rebounded to a distance of seven or eight feet before this clumsy detonator could do its work. When the explosion came, the intervening body of water prevented it from doing any great damage.

The *David* was not a true submarine but a surface torpedo boat, that could be submerged till only the funnel and a small pilot-house were exposed. A number of other *Davids* were built and operated by the Confederate States navy, but the first of them was the only one to accomplish anything.

The one real submarine possessed by the Confederacy was not a *David,* though she is usually so called. This was the C.S.S. *Hundley,* a hand-power " diving-boat "

C. S. S. *Hundley.*
The Only Submarine to sink a Hostile Warship before the Outbreak of the Present War.

not unlike Fulton's *Nautilus,* but very much clumsier and harder to manage. She had ballast tanks and a pair of diving-planes for steering her up and down, and she was designed to attack an enemy's ship by swimming under it, towing a torpedo that would explode on striking her opponent's keel.

Submarines in the Civil War

The *Hundley* was built at Mobile, Alabama, by the firm of Hundley and McKlintock, named for the senior partner, and brought to Charleston on a flatcar. There she was manned by a crew of nine volunteers, eight of whom sat in a row and turned the cranks on the propellor-shaft, while the ninth man steered. There was no conning-tower and the forward hatchway had to be left open for the helmsman to look out of while running on the surface. On the *Hundley's* first practice cruise, the wash from the paddle-wheels of a passing steamer poured suddenly down the open hatchway. Only the steersman and commanding officer, Lieutenant Payne, had time to save himself before the submarine sank, drowning the rest of her crew.

The boat was raised and Payne took her out with a new crew. This time a sudden squall sank her before they could close the hatches, and Payne escaped, with two of his men. He tried a third time, only to be capsized off Fort Sumter, with the loss of four of his crew. On the fourth trip, the hatches were closed, the tanks filled, and an attempt was made to navigate beneath the surface. But the *Hundley* dived too suddenly, stuck her nose deep into the muddy bottom, and stayed there till her entire crew were suffocated. On the fifth trial she became entangled in the cable of an anchored vessel, with the same result.

By this time the submarine's victims numbered thirty-five, and the Confederates had nicknamed her the "Peripatetic Coffin." But at the sixth call for volunteers, they still came forward. It was decided to risk no more lives on practice trips but to attack at once. In spite of the protests of Mr. Hundley, the designer of the craft, her latest and last commander, Lieutenant Dixon of the 21st South Carolina Infantry, was ordered by General Beauregard to use the vessel as a surface torpedo-boat, submerged to the hatch-coaming and with the hatches open. A spar-torpedo, to be exploded by pulling a trigger with a light line runing back into the boat, was mounted on the bow. Thus armed, and manned by Lieutenant Dixon, Captain Carlson, and five enlisted men of their regiment, the little *Hundley* put out over Charleston bar on the night of February 17, 1864, to attack some vessel of the blockading fleet. This proved to be the U.S.S. *Housatonic,* a fine new thirteen-gun corvette of 1264 tons. What followed is best described by Admiral David Porter in his " Naval History of the Civil War."

" At about 8.45 P.M., the officer of the deck on board the unfortunate vessel discovered something about 100 yards away, moving along the water. It came directly towards the ship, and within two minutes of the time it was first sighted was alongside. The cable was slipped, the engines backed, and all hands called to quarters. But it was too late — the torpedo struck the *Housatonic* just forward of the mainmast, on the starboard side, on a line with the magazine. The man who steered her (the *Hundley*) knew where the vital spots of the steamer were and he did his work well. When the explosion took place the ship trembled all over as if by the shock of an earthquake, and seemed to be lifted out of the water, and then sank stern foremost, heeling to port as she went down."

The *Hundley* was not seen after the explosion, and it

Submarines in the Civil War

was supposed that she had backed away and escaped. But when peace came, and Charleston Harbor was being cleared of the wrecks with which war had clogged it, the divers sent down to inspect the *Housatonic* found the *Hundley* lying beside her. Sucked in by the rush of the water through the hole her torpedo had made, she had been caught and dragged down by her own victim. All the *Hundley's* crew were found dead within her. So perished the first and last submarine to sink a hostile warship, before the outbreak of the present war. A smaller underwater boat of the same type was privately built at New Orleans at the beginning of the war, lost on her trial trip, and not brought up again till after peace was declared.

The North had a hand-power submarine, that was built at the Georgetown Navy Yard in 1862. It was designed by a Frenchman, whose name is now forgotten but who might have been a contemporary of Cornelius Van Drebel. Except that its hull was of steel instead of wood and greased leather, this first submarine of the United States navy was no better than an eel-boat of the seventeenth century. It was propelled by eight pairs of oars, with hinged blades that folded up like a book on the return stroke. The boat was thirty-five feet long and six in diameter, and was rowed by sixteen men. It was submerged by flooding ballast tanks. There was an oxygen tank and an apparatus for purifying the used air by blowing it over lime. A spar-torpedo was to be run out on rollers in the bow.

Ten thousand dollars was paid to the inventor of this medieval leftover, and he prudently left the country before he could be called on to operate it, though he had been promised a reward of five thousand dollars for every Confederate ironclad he succeeded in blowing up. Like the first *Monitor,* this nameless submarine was lost in a storm off Cape Hatteras, while being towed by a steamer.

After the loss of the *Housatonic,* the North built two semi-submersible steam torpedo-boats on the same idea as the *David,* but larger and faster. Both were armed with spar-torpedoes and fitted with ballast tanks to sink them very low in the water when they attacked. The smaller of the two, the *Stromboli,* could be submerged till only her pilot-house, smoke-stack, and one ventilator showed above the water. The other boat was called the *Spuyten Duyvil.* She could be sunk till her deck, which was covered with three inches of iron armor, was level with the water, but she bristled with masts, funnels, conning-towers, ventilators, and other excrescences that sprouted out of her hull at the most unexpected places. Neither of these craft was ever used in action.

CHAPTER V

THE WHITEHEAD TORPEDO

HOW best to float a charge of explosives against the hull of an enemy's ship and there explode it is the great problem of torpedo warfare. The spar-torpedo, that did such effective work in the Civil War, was little more than a can of gunpowder on the end of a stick. This stick or spar was mounted usually on the bow of a steam-launch, either partially submerged, like the *David*, or boldly running on the surface over log-booms and through a hail of bullets and grapeshot, as when Lieutenant Cushing sank the Confederate ironclad *Albemarle*. Once alongside, the spar-torpedo was run out to its full length, raised, depressed, and finally fired by pulling different ropes. So small was the chance of success and so great the danger to the launch's crew that naval officers and inventors all the world over sought constantly for some surer and safer way.

Early in the sixties, an Austrian artillery officer attached to the coast defenses conceived the idea of sending out the launch without a crew. He made some drawings of a big toy boat, to be driven by steam or hot air or even by clockwork, and steered from the shore by long ropes. As it would have no crew, this boat could carry the explosives in its hull, and the spars which were to project from it in all directions would carry no torpedoes themselves but would serve to explode the boat's cargo of guncotton by firing a pistol into it, as soon as one of the spars came into contact with the target. Before he could carry out his ideas any further, this officer died and his plans were turned over to Captain Lupuis of the Austrian navy. Lupuis experimented diligently with surface torpedoes till 1864, but found that he would have to discover some better steering-device than ropes from the shore and some other motive-power than steam or clockwork. So he consulted with Mr. Whitehead, the English manager of a firm of engine manufacturers at the seaport of Fiume.

Whitehead gave the torpedo a fish-shaped hull, so that it could run beneath instead of on the surface. For motive-power he used compressed air, which proved much superior to either steam or clockwork. And by improving its rudders, he enabled the little craft to keep its course without the aid of guide-ropes from the shore. The chief defect of the first Whitehead torpedoes, which were finished and tried in 1866, was that they kept bobbing to the surface, or else they would dive too deep and pass harmlessly under the target. To correct this defect, Whitehead invented by 1868 what he called the "balance chamber." Then, as now, each torpedo was divided into a number of separate compartments or chambers, and in one of these the inventor placed a most ingenious device for keeping the torpedo at a uniform depth. The contents of the balance-chamber was Whitehead's great secret, and it was not revealed to the public for twenty years.

The automobile or, as it was then called, the "submarine locomotive" torpedo was now a practicable,

The Whitehead Torpedo

though by no means perfected, weapon, and the Austrian naval authorities gave it a thorough trial at Fiume in 1868. Whitehead rigged up a crude ejecting tube on the bow of a gunboat, and successfully discharged two of his torpedoes at a yacht. The Austrian government promptly adopted the weapon, but could not obtain a monopoly of it, for Whitehead was a patriotic Englishman. The British admiralty invited him to England two years later, and after careful trials of its own, induced the English government to buy Whitehead's secret and manufacturing rights for $45,000. Other nations soon added "Whiteheads" to their navies, and in 1873 there was built in Norway a large, fast steam launch for the express purpose of carrying torpedoes and discharging them at an enemy. Every one began to build larger and swifter launches, till they evolved the torpedo-boat and the destroyer of to-day.

The torpedo itself has undergone a similar development in size and efficiency. The difference between the Whiteheads of forty-five years ago and those of to-day is strikingly shown in the following table:

	Length, Feet	Diameter, Inches	Charge, Pounds	Range, Yards	Speed, Knots
British Naval Torpedoes of 1870					
Large	14	16	67 guncotton	600	7.5
Small	13	10.58 in. 14	18 dynamite	200	8.5
British Naval Torpedoes of 1915					
Large	21	21	330 guncotton	12,000	48
Small	18	18	200 guncotton	16,000	36

The length of a large modern torpedo, it will be observed, is only three inches less than that of Fulton's famous submarine boat of 1801. A Whitehead torpedo is really a small automatic submarine, steered and controlled by the most ingenious and sensitive machinery, as surely as if it were manned by a crew of Lilliputian seamen.

Projecting from the head is the "striker," a rod which, when the torpedo runs into anything hard, is driven back in against a detonator or "percussion-cap" of fulminate of mercury. Just as the hammer of a toy "cap-pistol" explodes a paper cap, so the sudden shock of the in-driven striker explodes the fulminate, which is instantly expanded to more than two thousand times its former size. This, in turn, gives a severe blow to the surrounding "primer" of dry guncotton. The primer is exploded, and by its own expansion sets off the main charge of several hundred pounds of wet guncotton.

The reason for this is that though wet guncotton is safe to handle because a very great shock is required to make it explode, dry guncotton is much less so, while a shell or torpedo filled with fulminate of mercury would be more dangerous to its owners than to their enemies, because the slightest jar might set it off prematurely. Every precaution is taken to prevent a torpedo's exploding too soon and damaging the vessel from which it is fired.

When the torpedo is shot out of the tube, by compressed air, like a pea from a pea-shooter, the striker is held fast by the "jammer": a small propellor-shaped collar, whose blades begin to revolve as soon as they

The Whitehead Torpedo

strike the water, till the collar has unscrewed itself and dropped off after the torpedo has traveled about forty feet. A copper pin that runs through the striker-rod is not removed but must be broken short off by a blow of considerable violence, such as would be given by running into a ship's hull. As a third safeguard, there is a strong safety-catch, that must be released by hand, just before the torpedo is placed in the tube.

The explosive charge of two or three hundred pounds of wet guncotton is called the "war-head." In peace and for target-practice it is replaced by a dummy head of thick steel. The usual target is the space between two buoys moored a ship's length or less apart. At the end of a practice run, the torpedo rises to the surface, where it can be recovered and used again. This is distinctly worth while, for a modern torpedo costs more than seven thousand dollars.

Back of the war-head is the air-chamber, that contains the motive-power of this miniature submarine. The air is either packed into it by powerful pumps, on shore or shipboard, or else drawn from one of the storage flasks of compressed air, a number of which are carried on every submarine. The air-chamber of a modern torpedo is charged at a pressure of from 2000 to 2500 pounds per square inch. As the torpedo leaves the tube, a lever on its back is struck and knocked over by a little projecting piece of metal, and the starting-valve of the air-chamber is opened. But if the compressed air were allowed to reach and start the engines at once, they would begin to revolve the propellors while they were still in the air inside the tube. This would cause the screws to "race," or spin round too rapidly and perhaps break off. So there is a "delaying-valve," which keeps the air away from the engines till another valve-lever is swung over by the impact of the water against a little metal flap.

As the compressed air rushes through the pipe from the chamber to the engine-room, it passes through a "reducing-valve," which keeps it from spurting at the start and lagging at the finish. By supplying the air to the engines at a reduced but uniform pressure, this device enables the torpedo to maintain the same speed throughout the run. At the same time the compressed air is heated by a small jet of burning oil, with a consequent increase in pressure, power, and speed, estimated at 30 per cent. All these devices are kept not in the air-chamber itself but in the next compartment, the balance-chamber.

Here is the famous little machine, once a close-kept secret but now known to all the world, that holds the torpedo at any desired depth. Think of a push-button, working in a tube open to the sea, with the water pressure pushing the button in and a spiral spring inside shoving it out. This push-button — called a "hydrostatic valve" — is connected by a system of levers with the two diving-planes or horizontal rudders that steer the torpedo up or down. By turning a screw, the spring can be adjusted to exert a force equal to the pressure of the water at any given depth. If the torpedo dives too deep, the increased water-pressure forces in the valve, moves the levers, raises the diving-planes, and steers the torpedo towards the surface. As the water pressure grows less, the spring forces out the valve, depresses the diving-planes, and brings the miniature submarine down to its proper depth again. When his torpedoes grew too big to be controlled by the comparatively feeble force exerted by the hydrostatic valve, Whitehead invented the "servo-motor": an auxiliary, compressed-air engine, less than five inches long, sensitive enough to respond to the slightest movement of the valve levers but strong enough to steer the largest torpedo, exactly as the steam steering-gear moves the huge rudder of an ocean liner.

There is also a heavy pendulum, swinging fore and aft and attached to the diving-planes, that checks any sudden up-or-down movement of the torpedo by inclining the planes and restoring the horizontal position.

Next comes the engine-room, with its three-cylinder motor, capable of developing from thirty-five to fifty-five horse-power. The exhaust air from the engine passes out through the stern in a constant stream of bubbles, leaving a broad white streak on the surface of the water as the torpedo speeds to its mark.

The aftermost compartment is called the buoyancy chamber. Besides adding to the floatability of the torpedo, this space also holds the engine shaft and the gear attaching it to the twin propellors. The first Whiteheads were single-screw boats. But the revolution of the propellor in one direction set up a reaction that caused the torpedo itself to partially revolve or heel over in the other, disturbing its rudders and swerving it from its course. This reaction is neutralized by using two propellers, one revolving to the right, the other to the left.

Instead of being placed side by side, as on a steamer, they are mounted one behind the other, with the shaft of one revolving inside the hollow shaft of the other, and in the opposite direction.

Long after they could be depended on to keep a proper depth, the Whiteheads and other self-propelled torpedoes were liable to swing suddenly to port or starboard, or even turn completely round. During the war between Chile and Peru, in 1879, the Peruvian ironclad *Huascar* discharged an automobile torpedo that went halfway to the target, changed its mind, and was coming back to blow up its owners when an officer swam out to meet it and succeeded in turning it aside, for the torpedoes of that time were slow and small as well as erratic.

Nowadays a torpedo is kept on a straight course by a gyroscope placed in the buoyancy chamber. Nearly every boy knows the gyroscopic top, like a little flywheel, that you can spin on the edge of a tumbler. The upper part of this toy is a heavy little metal wheel, and if you try to push it over while it is spinning, it resists and pushes back, as if it were alive. A similar wheel, weighing about two pounds, is placed in the buoyancy chamber of a Whitehead. When the torpedo starts, it releases either a powerful spring or an auxiliary compressed air engine that sets the gyroscope to spinning at more than two thousand revolutions a minute. It revolves vertically, in the fore-and-aft line of the torpedo, and is mounted on a pivoted stand. If the torpedo deviates from its straight course, the gyroscope does not, and the consequent change in their relative positions brings the flywheel into contact with a lever running to the servo-

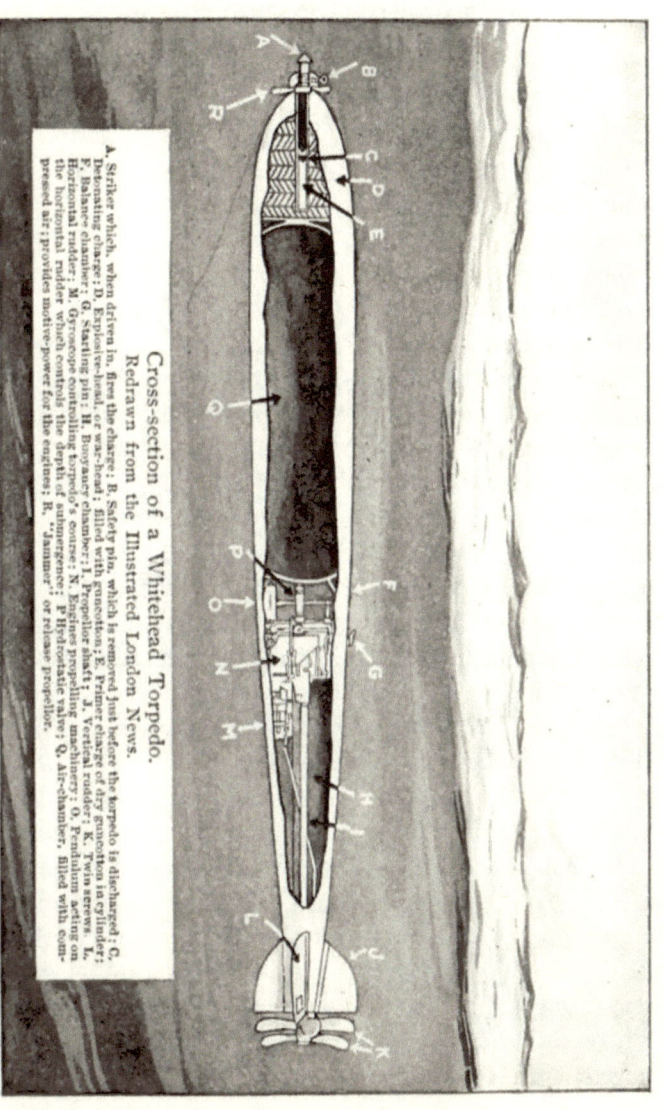

Cross-section of a Whitehead Torpedo.
Redrawn from the Illustrated London News.

A, Striker which, when driven in, fires the charge; B, Safety pin, which is removed just before the torpedo is discharged; C, Detonating charge; D, Explosive-head, or war-head; E, Primer charge of dry guncotton in a cylinder; F, Balance chamber; G, Starting pin; H, Buoyancy chamber; I, Propeller shaft; J, Vertical charge of dry guncotton in a cylinder; K, Twin screws; L, Horizontal rudder; M, Gyroscope controlling torpedo's course; N, Engines propelling machinery; O, Pendulum acting on the horizontal rudder which controls the depth of submergence; P Hydrostatic valve; Q, Air-chamber, filled with compressed air, provides motive power for the engines; R, "Jammer" or release propeller.

motor that controls the two vertical rudders, which soon set the torpedo right again.

Thus guided and driven, a modern torpedo speeds swiftly and surely to its target, there to blow itself into a thousand pieces, with a force sufficient to sink a ship a thousand times its size.

The Whitehead is used by every navy in the world except the German, which has its own torpedo: the "Schwartzkopf." This, however, is practicaly identical with the Whitehead, except that its hull is made of bronze instead of steel and its war-head is charged with trinitrotuluol, or T.N.T., a much more powerful explosive than guncotton.

After the Russo-Japanese War, when several Russian battleships kept afloat although they had been struck by Japanese torpedoes, many naval experts declared that an exploding war-head spent most of its energy in throwing a great column of water up into the air, instead of blowing in the side of the ship. So Commander Davis of the United States navy invented his "gun-torpedo." This is like a Whitehead in every respect except that instead of a charge of guncotton it carries in its head a short eight-inch cannon loaded with an armor-piercing shell and a small charge of powder. In this type of torpedo, the impact of the striker against the target serves to fire the gun. The shell then passes easily through the thin side of the ship below the armor-belt and through any protecting coal-bunkers and bulkheads it may encounter, till it reaches the ship's vitals, where it is exploded by the delayed action of an adjustable time-fuse. What would happen if it burst in a magazine or boiler-room is best

The Whitehead Torpedo 53

left to the imagination. Several Davis gun-torpedoes have been built and used against targets with very satisfactory results, but they have not yet been used in actual warfare.

Mr. Edward F. Chandler, M.E., one of the foremost torpedo-experts in America, is dissatisfied with the com-

Courtesy of the Electric Boat Company.

Davis Gun-Torpedo after discharge, showing eight-inch gun forward of air-flask.

pressed-air driven gyroscope, both because it does not begin to revolve till after the torpedo has been launched and perhaps deflected from its true course, and because it cannot be made to spin continuously throughout the long run of a modern torpedo. He proposes to remove the compressed-air servo-motors, both for this purpose and for controlling the horizontal-rudders by the hydrostatic valve, and replace them with an electrical-driven gyroscope and depth-gear. The increased efficiency of the latter would enable him to get rid of the heavy, uncertain pendulum, thus allowing for the weight of the storage batteries. Mr. Chandler declares that his electrically-controlled torpedo can be lowered over the side of a small boat, headed in any desired direction, and started, without any launching-tube.[1]

Though the automobile torpedo has been brought to so

Courtesy of the Electric Boat Company.
Effect of Davis Gun-Torpedo on a specially-constructed target.

high a state of perfection, the original idea of steering from the shore has not been abandoned. The Brennan and Sims-Edison controllable torpedoes were driven and steered by electricity, receiving the current through wires trailed astern and carrying little masts and flags above the surface to guide the operator on shore. But these also served as a warning to the enemy and gave him too good a chance either to avoid the torpedo or destroy it with machine-gun fire. Then, too, the trailing wires reduced

[1] See the "Scientific American," August 7, 1915.

The Whitehead Torpedo

its speed and were always liable to get tangled in the propellors. Controllable torpedoes of this type were abandoned before the outbreak of the present war and will probably never be used in action.

A new and more promising sort of controllable torpedo was immediately suggested by the invention of wireless telegraphy. Many inventors have been working to perfect such a weapon, and a young American engineer, Mr. John Hays Hammond, Jr., seems to have succeeded. From his wireless station on shore, Mr. Hammond can make a small, crewless electric launch run hither and yon as he pleases about the harbor of Gloucester, Massachusetts. The commander and many of the officers of the United States coast artillery corps have carefully inspected and tested this craft, which promises to be the forerunner of a new and most formidable species of coast defense torpedo.

CHAPTER VI

FREAKS AND FAILURES

DURING the half-century following the death of Fulton, scarcely a year went by without the designing or launching of a new man-power submarine. Some of these boats, notably those of the Bavarian Wilhelm Bauer, were surprisingly good, others were most amazingly bad, but none of them led to anything better. Inventor after inventor wasted his substance discovering what Van Drebel, Bushnell, and Fulton had known before him, only to die and have the same facts painfully rediscovered by some one on the other side of the earth.

A striking example of this lack of progress is Halstead's *Intelligent Whale*. Built for the United States navy at New York, in the winter of 1864–5, this craft is no more modern and much less efficient than Fulton's *Nautilus* of 1801. The *Intelligent Whale* is a fat, cigar-shaped, iron vessel propelled by a screw cranked by manpower and submerged by dropping two heavy anchors to the bottom and then warping the boat down to any desired depth. A diver can then emerge from a door in the submarine's bottom, to place a mine under a hostile ship. It was not until 1872 that the *Intelligent Whale* was sent on a trial trip in Newark Bay. Manned by an utterly inexperienced and very nervous crew, the clumsy submarine got entirely out of control and had to be hauled up by a cable that had been thoughtfully attached to her before she went down. Fortunately no lives had been lost, but the wildest stories were told and printed, till the imaginary death-roll ran up to forty-nine. The *Intelligent Whale* was hauled up on dry land and can still be seen on exhibition at the corner of Third Street and Perry Avenue in the Brooklyn Navy Yard.

Lack of motive-power was the reason why man-sized submarines lagged behind their little automatic brethren, the Whitehead torpedoes. Compressed air was just the thing for a spurt, but when two Frenchmen, Captain Bourgois and M. Brun, built the *Plongeur,* a steel submarine 146 feet long and 12 feet in diameter, at Rochefort in 1863, and fitted it with an eighty-horse-power, compressed-air engine, they discovered that the storage-flasks emptied themselves too quickly to permit a voyage of any length.

The *Plongeur* also proved that while you can sink a boat to the bottom by filling her ballast-tanks or make her rise to the surface by emptying them, you cannot make her float suspended between two bodies of water except by holding her there by some mechanical means. Without anything of the kind, the *Plongeur* kept bouncing up and down like a rubber ball. Once her inventors navigated her horizontally for some distance, only to find that she had been sliding on her stomach along the soft muddy bottom of a canal. Better results were obtained after the *Plongeur* was fitted with a crude pair of diving-planes. But the inefficiency of her compressed-air engine caused her to be condemned and turned into a water tank.

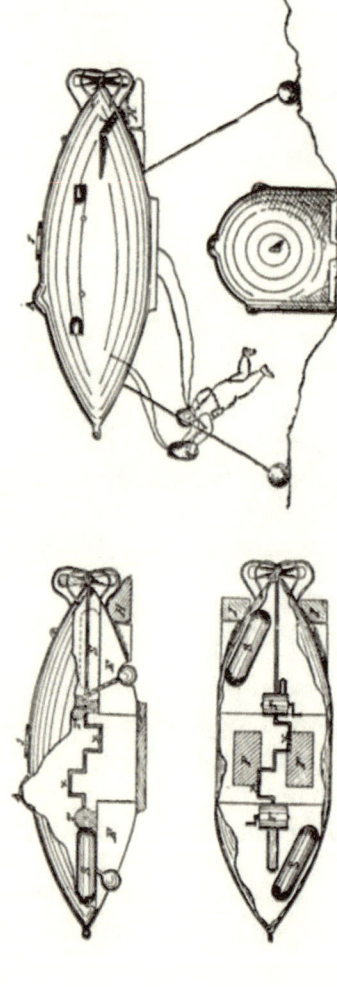

The *Intelligent Whale.*

Drawn by Lieutenant F. M. Barber, U. S. N., in 1875.

Freaks and Failures

Electricity was first applied in 1861 by another Frenchman, named Olivier Riou. This is the ideal motive-power for underwater boats, and it was at this time that Jules Verne described the ideal submarine in his immortal story of "Twenty Thousand Leagues Under the Sea." But before we can have a *Nautilus* like Captain Nemo's we must discover an electric storage battery of unheard-of lightness and capacity.

There was a great revival of French interest in electric submarines after Admiral Aube, who was a lifelong

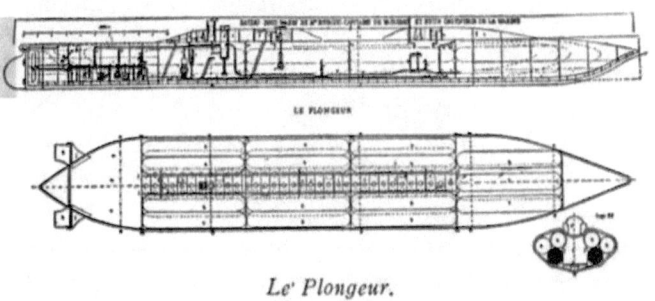

Le Plongeur.

submarine "fan," became minister of marine in 1886. In spite of much ridicule and opposition, he authorized the construction of a small experimental vessel of this type called the *Gymnote*. She was a wild little thing that did everything short of turning somersaults when she dived, but she was enough of a success to be followed by a larger craft named, after the great engineer who had designed her predecessor, the *Gustave Zédé*.

"The history of the *Gustave Zédé* shows how much in earnest the French were in the matter of submarines. When she was first launched she was a failure in almost every respect, and it was only after some years, during which many alterations and improvements were carried out, that she became a serviceable craft. At first nothing would induce the *Gustave Zédé* to quit the surface, and when at last she did plunge she did it so effectually that she went down to the bottom in 10 fathoms of water at an angle of 30 degrees. The committee of engineers were on board at the time, and it speaks well for their patriotism that they did not as a result of their unpleasant experience condemn the *Gustave Zédé* and advise the government to spend no more money on submarine craft." [1]

Twenty-nine other electric submarines were built for the French navy between 1886 and 1901. During the same period, a French gentleman named M. Goubet built and experimented with two very small electric submarines, each of which was manned by two men, who sat back to back on a sort of settee stuffed with machinery. Little or big, all these French boats had the same fatal defect: lack of power. Their storage batteries, called on to propel them above, as well as below, the surface, became exhausted after a few hours' cruising. They were as useless for practical naval warfare as an electric runabout would be to haul guns or carry supplies in Flanders.

But if compressed-air and electricity were too quickly exhausted, gasoline or petroleum was even less practicable for submarine navigation. To set an oil-engine, that derives its power from the explosion of a mixture of oil-vapor and air, at work in a small closed space like the interior of a submarine, would soon make it uninhabit-

[1] Herbert C. Fyfe, "Submarine Warfare," p. 269.

able. While Mr. Holland was puzzling how to overcome this difficulty, in the middle eighties, a Swedish inventor named Nordenfeldt was building submarines to be run by steam-power.

Mr. Nordenfeldt, who is remembered to-day as the inventor of the famous gun that bears his name, had taken up the idea of an English clergyman named Garett, who in 1878 had built a submarine called the *Resurgam,* or "I Shall Rise." Garett's second boat, built a year later, had a steam-engine. When the vessel was submerged, the smoke-stack was closed by a sliding panel, the furnace doors were shut tight, and the engine run by the steam given off by a big tank full of bottled-up hot water. Nordenfeldt improved this system till his hot-water tanks gave off enough steam to propel his boat beneath the surface for a distance of fourteen miles.

He also rediscovered and patented Bushnell's device for submerging a boat by pushing it straight down and holding it under with a vertical propellor. His first submarine had two of these, placed in sponsons or projections on either side of the center of the hull. The Nordenfeldt boats, with their cigar-shaped hulls and projecting smoke-stacks, looked like larger editions of the Civil War *Davids,* and like them, could be submerged by taking in water-ballast till only a strip of deck with the funnel and conning-tower projected above the surface. Then the vertical propellors would begin to revolve and force the boat straight down on an even keel. Mr. Nordenfeldt insisted with great earnestness that this was the only safe and proper way to submerge a submarine. If you tried to steer it downward with any kind of driving-planes, he declared, then the boat was liable to keep on descending, before you could pull its head up, till it either struck the bottom or was crushed in by the pressure of too great a depth of water. There was a great deal of truth in this, but Mr. Nordenfeldt failed to reaiize that if one of his vertical propellors pushed only a little harder

Steam Submarine *Nordenfeldt II,* at Constantinople, 1887. Observe vertical-acting propellors on deck.
Reproduced from "Submarine Navigation, Past and Present" by Alan H. Burgoyne, by permission of E. P. Dutton & Company

than the other, then the keel of his own submarine was going to be anything but even.

The first Nordenfeldt boat was launched in 1886 and bought by Greece, after a fairly successful trial in the Bay of Salamis. Two larger and more powerful submarines: *Nordenfeldt II* and *III,* were promptly ordered by Greece's naval rival Turkey. Each of these was 125 feet long, or nearly twice the length of the Greek boat, and each carried its two vertical propellors on deck, one forward and the other aft. Both boats were shipped in sections to Constantinople in 1887, but only *Nordenfeldt II* was put together and tried. She was one of the first submarines to be armed with a bow torpedo-tube for discharging Whiteheads, and as a surface torpedo-boat, she was a distinct success. But when they tried to navigate her under water there was a circus.

No sooner did one of the crew take two steps forward in the engine-room than down went the bow. The hot water in the boilers and the cold water in the ballast-tanks ran downhill, increasing the slant still further. English engineers, Turkish sailors, monkey-wrenches, hot ashes, Whitehead torpedoes, and other movables came tumbling after, till the submarine was nearly standing on her head, with everything inside packed into the bow like toys in the toe of a Christmas stocking. The little vertical propellors pushed and pulled and the crew clawed their way aft, till suddenly up came her head, down went her tail, and everything went gurgling and clattering down to the other end. *Nordenfeldt II* was a perpetual see-saw, and no mortal power could keep her on an even keel. Once they succeeded in steadying her long enough to fire a torpedo. Where it went to, no man can tell, but the sudden lightening of the bow and the recoil of the discharge made the submarine rear up and sit down so hard that she began to sink stern foremost. The water was blown out of her ballast tanks by steam-pressure, and the main engine started full speed ahead, till she shot up to the surface like a flying-fish. The Turkish naval authorities, watching the trials from the shores of the Golden Horn, were so impressed by these antics that they bought the boat. But it was impossible to keep a crew on her, for every native engineer or seaman who was sent on board prudently deserted on the first dark night. So the *Nordenfeldt II* rusted away till she fell to pieces, long before the Allied fleets began the forcing of the Dardanelles.

Fantastic though their performances seem to us today, these submarines represent the best work of some of the most capable inventors and naval engineers of the nineteenth century. With them deserve to be mentioned the boats of the Russian Drzewiecki and the Spaniard Peral. Failures though they were, they taught the world many valuable lessons about the laws controlling the actions of submerged bodies.

But many of the underwater craft invented between 1850 and 1900 can be classified only as freaks. Most of them, fortunately, were designed but never built, and those that were launched miraculously refrained from drowning any of their crews. There were submarines armed with steam-driven gimlets: the

> "nimble tail,
> Made like an auger, with which tail she wriggles,
> Betwixt the ribs of a ship and sinks it straight,"

that Ben Jonson playfully ascribed to Van Drebel. Dr. Lacomme, in 1869, proposed a submarine railroad from Calais to Dover, with tracks laid on the bottom of the Channel and cars that could cast off their wheels and

Bauer's Submarine Concert, Cronstadt Harbor, 1855. See footnote, page 120
An original drawing by the author, Alan H. Burgoyne; reproduced from "Submarine Navigation, Past and Present,"
by permission of E. P. Dutton & Company.

rise to the surface in case of accident. Lieutenant André Constantin designed, during the siege of Paris, a boat to be submerged by drawing in pistons working in large cylinders open to the water. A vessel was actually built on this principle in England in 1888, and submerged in Tilbury Docks, where the soft mud at the bottom choked the cylinders so that the pistons could not be driven out again and the boat was brought up with considerable difficulty. Two particularly delirious inventors claimed that their submarines could also be used as dirigible balloons. Boucher's underwater boat of 1886 was to have gills like a fish, so that it need never rise to the surface for air, and was further adorned with spring-buffers on the bottom, oars, a propellor under the center of the keel, and a movable tail for sculling the vessel forward. There were submarines with paddle-wheels, submarines with fins, and submarines with wings. A Venezuelan dentist, Señor Lacavalerier, invented a double-hulled, cigar-shaped boat, whose outer hull was threaded like a screw, and by revolving round the fixed inner hull, bored its way through the water. But he had been anticipated and outdone by Apostoloff, a Russian, who not only designed a submarine on the same principle but intended it to carry a large cabin suspended on davits above the surface of the water, and declared that his vessel would cross the Atlantic at an average speed of 111 knots an hour.

As late as 1898 the Spanish government, neglecting the promising little electric boat built ten years before by Señor Peral, was experimenting with two highly impossible submarines, one of which was to be propelled

Apostoloff's Proposed Submarine.

An original drawing by the author, Alan H. Burgoyne; reproduced from "Submarine Navigation, Past and Present," by permission of E. P. Dutton & Company.

by a huge clock-spring, while the other was perfectly round. Needless to say, neither the sphere nor the toy boat ever encountered the American fleet.

At the same time, the United States government declined to accept the war services of the already practicable boats of the two American inventors who were about to usher in the present era of submarine warfare: Simon Lake and John P. Holland.

CHAPTER VII

JOHN P. HOLLAND

WHEN the *Merrimac* rammed the *Cumberland,* burned the *Congress,* and was fought to a standstill next day by the little *Monitor,* all the world realized that there had been a revolution in naval warfare. The age of the wooden warship was gone forever, the day of the ironclad had come. And a twenty-year-old Irish school-teacher began to wonder what would be the next revolution; what new craft might be invented that would dethrone the ironclad. This young Irishman's name was John P. Holland, and he decided to devote his life to the perfection of the submarine.

Like Robert Fulton, Admiral Von Tirpitz, and the Frenchman who built the *Rotterdam Boat* in 1652, Holland relied on submarines to break the power of the British fleet. Though born a British subject, in the little village of Liscannor, County Clare in the year 1842, he had seen too many of his fellow countrymen starved to death or driven into exile not to hate the stupid tyranny that characterized England's rule of Ireland in those bitter, far-off days. He longed for the day of Ireland's independence, and that day seemed to be brought much nearer by the American Civil War.. Not only had many thousand brave Irish-Americans become trained veterans but Great Britain and the United States had been brought to the verge of war by the sinking of American ships by the *Alabama* and other British-built, Confederate commerce-destroyers. When that Anglo-American war broke out, there would be an army ready to come over and free Ireland — if only the troublesome British navy could be put out of the way. And already the English were launching ironclad after ironclad to replace their now useless steam-frigates and ships-of-the-line. It is no use trying to outbuild or outfight the British navy above

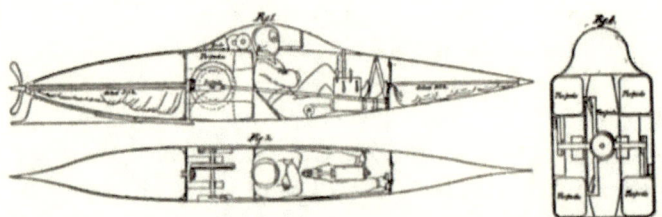

The *Holland No. 1*. Designed to carry a torpedo and fix it to the bottom of a ship, on the general principle of Bushnell's *Turtle*. Drawn by Lieutenant F. M. Barber, U. S. N., in 1875.

water, and John P. Holland realized this in 1862, as several kings and emperors have, before or since.

Though his friends in Cork kept laughing at him, Holland worked steadily on his plans for a submarine boat, throughout the sixties. Presently he came to America and obtained a job as school-teacher in Paterson, New Jersey. There he built and launched his first submarine in 1875. It was a sharp-pointed, little, cigar-shaped affair, only sixteen feet long and two feet in diameter amidships. This craft was designed to carry a torpedo and fix it to the bottom of a ship, on the general principle of Bushnell's *Turtle*. It was divided into four compartments, with air-chambers fore and aft. Air-pipes led to where Holland sat in the middle, with his head in a respirator shaped like a diver's helmet, and his feet working pedals that turned the propellor.

There was nothing revolutionary about this *Holland No. 1*. A similar underwater bicycle is said to have been invented by Alvary Templo in 1826, and Drzewiecki used one at Odessa in 1877. But Holland used his to teach himself how to build something better. Just as the Wright brothers learned how to build and fly aeroplanes by coasting down through the air from the tops of the Kitty Hawk sand-hills in their motorless "glider," so John P. Holland found how to make and navigate submarines by diving under the surface of the Passaic River and adjacent waters, and swimming around there in his *No. 1* and her successors.

The *Holland No. 2* was launched in 1877 and became immediately and prophetically stuck in the mud. She had a double hull, the space between being used as a ballast-tank, whose contents leaked constantly into the interior, and she was driven intermittently by a four horse-power petroleum engine of primitive design. After a series of trials that entertained his neighbors and taught the inventor that the best place for a single horizontal rudder is the stern, Holland took the engine out of the boat and sank her under the Falls Bridge, where she lies to this day.

He then entered into negotiations with the Fenian Brotherhood, a secret society organized for the purpose of setting up an Irish republic by militant methods.

Though not a Fenian himself, Holland was thoroughly in sympathy with the brotherhood, and offered to show them how they could get round, or rather under, the British navy. You may have seen a once-familiar lithograph of a green-painted superdreadnought of strange design flying the Crownless Harp, and named the Irish battleship *Emerald Isle*. The only real Irish warships of modern times, however, were the two submarines Holland persuaded the Fenians to have him build at their expense.

Rear-Admiral Philip Hichborn, former Chief Constructor, U.S.N., said of these two boats:

"She (the earlier one) was the first submarine since Bushnell's time employing water ballast and always retaining buoyancy, in which provision was made to insure a fixed center of gravity and a fixed absolute weight. Moreover, she was the first buoyant submarine to be steered down and up in the vertical plane by horizontal-rudder action as she was pushed forward by her motor, instead of being pushed up and down by vertical-acting mechanism.[1] Her petroleum engine, provided for motive-power and for charging her compressed-air flasks, was inefficient, and the boat therefore failed as a practical craft; but in her were demonstrated all the chief principles of successful, brain-directed, submarine navigation. In 1881, Holland turned out a larger and better boat in which he led the world far and away in the

[1] But Fulton's *Nautilus* could not possibly have made the dives with which she is credited except by the use of the horizontal rudders which she possessed in conjunction with the push of her man-power propellor. Holland had carefully studied the plans and letters of Bushnell and Fulton.

solution of submarine problems, and for a couple of years demonstrated that he could perfectly control his craft in the vertical plane. Eventually, through financial complications, she was taken to New Haven, where she now is."

Political as well as financial complications caused the

The *Fenian Ram*.
(Photographed by Mr. Simon Lake, in the shed at New Haven.)

internment of this submarine, which a New York reporter, with picturesque inaccuracy, called the *Fenian Ram*. The Irish at home were by this time thinking less of fighting for independence and more for peacefully obtaining home rule, while the arbitration and payment of the "Alabama claims" by Great Britain had removed all danger of a war between that country and the United

States. Under these circumstances, many of the Fenians felt that it was wasted money for their society to spend any more of its funds on warships it could never find use for. This led to dissensions which culminated in a party of Fenians seizing the *Ram* and taking it to a shed on the premises of one of their members at New Haven, where it has remained ever since.

But the construction and performances of this submarine, and of several others which he soon afterwards built for himself, won Holland such a reputation that when Secretary Whitney decided in 1888 that submarines would be a good thing for the United States navy, the great Philadelphia ship-building firm of Cramps submitted two designs: Holland's and Nordenfeldt's, and the former won the award. But after nearly twelve months had been spent in settling preliminary details, and when a contract for building an experimental boat was just about to be awarded, there came a change of administration and the matter was dropped.

This was a great disappointment for Holland, and the next four or five years were lean ones for the inventor. He had built five boats and designed a sixth without their having brought him a cent of profit. It was not until March 3, 1893, that Congress appropriated the money for the construction of an experimental submarine, and inventors were invited to submit their designs. By this time John P. Holland had not only spent all his own money, but all he could borrow from his relatives and friends. To make matters worse, the country was then passing through a financial panic, when very few people had any money to lend or invest. And all the security

Holland could offer was his faith in the future of the submarine, which at that time was a stock joke of the comic papers, together with those other two crack-brained projects, the flying-machine and the horseless carriage.

"I know I can win that competition and build that boat for the Government," said Holland to a young lawyer whom he had met at lunch in a downtown New York restaurant, "if I can only raise the money to pay the fees and other expenses. I need exactly $347.19."

"What do you want the nineteen cents for?" asked the other.

"To buy a certain kind of ruler I need for drawing my plans."

"If you've figured it out as closely as all that," replied the lawyer, "I'll take a chance and lend you the money."

He did so, receiving in exchange a large block of stock in the new-formed Holland Torpedo-boat Company. To-day his stock is worth several million dollars.

Mr. Holland won the competition and after two years' delay his company began the construction of the *Plunger*. This submarine was to be propelled by steam while running on the surface and by storage-batteries when submerged. Double propulsion of this type had been first installed by a Southerner named Alstitt on a submarine he built at Mobile, Alabama, in 1863, and theoretically discussed in a book written in 1887 by Commander Hovgaard of the Danish navy. Though a great improvement on any type of single propulsion, this system had many drawbacks, the chief of which was the length of time — from fifteen to thirty minutes — that it took for the oil-burning surface engine to cool and rid itself of hot gases before it was safe to seal the funnel and dive. Though the *Plunger* was launched in 1897, she was never finished, for Mr. Holland foresaw her defects. He persuaded the Government to let his company pay back the money already spent on the *Plunger* and build an entirely new boat.

Holland No. 8 was built accordingly, but failed to work properly. Finally came the ninth and last of her line, the first of the modern submarines, the world-famous *Holland*.

She was a chunky little porpoise of a boat, 10 feet 7 inches deep and only 53 feet 10 inches long, and looking even shorter and thicker than she was because of the narrow, comb-like superstructure running fore and aft along the deck. But her shape and dimensions were the results of twenty-five years' experience. Built at Mr. Lewis Nixon's shipyards at Elizabethport, New Jersey, the *Holland* was launched in the early spring of 1898, between the blowing-up of the *Maine* and the outbreak of the Spanish-American War. But though John P. Holland repeatedly begged to be allowed to take his submarine into Santiago Harbor and torpedo Cervera's fleet, the naval authorities at Washington were too conservative-minded to let him try.

"United States warship goes down with all hands!" the small boys (I was one of them) used to shout at this time, and then explain that it was only another dive of the "Holland submarine." Strictly speaking, the *Holland* was not a United States warship till October 13, 1900, when she was formally placed in commission

Courtesy of the Electric Boat Company

U. S. S. *Holland*, in Drydock with the Russian Battleship *Retvizan*.

under the command of Lieutenant Harry H. Caldwell, who had been on her during many of the exhaustive series of trials in which the little undersea destroyer proved to even the most conservative officers of our navy that the day of the submarine had come at last.

Propelled on the surface by a fifty horse-power gasoline motor, the *Holland* had a cruising radius of 1500 miles at a speed of seven knots an hour. Submerged, she was driven by electric storage-batteries. This effective combination of oil-engines with an electric motor is one of John P. Holland's great discoveries, and is used in every submarine to-day. When her tanks were filled till her deck was flush with the water, and the two horizontal rudders at the stern began to steer her downwards, the *Holland* could dive to a depth of twenty-eight feet in five seconds. She had no periscope, for that instrument was then crude and unsatisfactory. To take aim, the captain of the *Holland* had to make a quick "porpoise dive," up to the surface and down again, exposing the conning-tower for the few seconds needed to take aim and judge the distance to the target. Though by this means the *Holland* succeeded in getting within striking-distance of the *Kearsarge* and the *New York* without being detected, during the summer manœuvers of the Atlantic fleet off Newport in 1900, it has proved fatal to the only submarine that has tried it in actual warfare (see page 160).

Less than half the length of the *Nordenfeldt II*, the *Holland* did not pitch or see-saw when submerged. Each of her crew of six sat on a low stool beside the machinery he was to operate, and there was no moving about when below the surface. Neither did the boat stand on her tail when a torpedo was discharged from the bow-tube, for the loss of weight was immediately compensated by admitting an equivalent amount of water into a tank. Originally the *Holland* had a stern torpedo-tube as well, besides a pneumatic gun for throwing eighty pounds of dynamite half a mile through the air, but these were later removed.

How the *Holland* impressed our naval officers at that time is best shown in the oft-quoted testimony of Admiral Dewey before the naval committee of the House of Representatives in 1900.

" Gentlemen, I saw the operation of the boat down off Mount Vernon the other day. Several members of this committee were there. I think we were all very much impressed with its performance. My aid, Lieutenant Caldwell, was on board. The boat did everything that the owners proposed to do. I said then, and I have said it since, that if they had had two of those things at Manila, I could never have held it with the squadron I had. The moral effect — to my mind, it is infinitely superior to mines or torpedoes or anything of the kind. With those craft moving under water it would wear people out. With two of those in Galveston all the navies of the world could not blockade the place."

The *Holland* was purchased by the United States Government on April 11, 1900, for $150,000. She had cost her builders, exclusive of any office expenses or salaries of officers, $236,615.43. But it had been a profitable investment for the Holland Torpedo-boat Company, for on August 25, the United States navy contracted with it for the construction of six more submarines. And in the autumn of the same year, though it was not announced to the public till March 1, 1901, five other

John P. Holland.

Hollands were ordered through the agency of Vickers Sons, and Maxim by the British admiralty. Soon every maritime nation was either buying *Hollands* or paying royalties on the inventor's patents, and building bigger, faster, better submarines every year.

The original *Holland* had outlived her fighting value when she was condemned by Secretary Daniels in June, 1915, to be broken up and sold as junk. There is still room in the Brooklyn Navy Yard for that worthless and meaningless relic, the *Intelligent Whale,* but there was none for the *Holland* submarine, whose place in history is with the *Clairmont* and the *Monitor.*

John P. Holland withdrew in 1904 from the Holland Torpedo-boat Company, which has since become merged with the Electric Boat Company, that builds most of the submarines for the United States navy, and many for the navies of foreign powers. Like most other great inventive geniuses, Holland was not a trained engineer, and it was perhaps inevitable that disputes should have arisen between him and his associates as to the carrying out of his ideas. His last years were embittered by the belief that the submarines of to-day were distorted and worthless developments of his original type. Whether or not he was mistaken, only time can tell. That to John P. Holland, more than to any other man since David Bushnell and Robert Fulton, the world owes the modern submarine, cannot be denied. His death, on August 12, 1914, was but little noticed in the turmoil and confusion of the first weeks of the great European War. But when the naval histories of that war are written, his name will not be forgotten.

CHAPTER VIII

THE LAKE SUBMARINES

JOHN P. HOLLAND was not the only inventor who responded to the invitation of the United States navy department to submit designs for a proposed submarine boat in 1893. That invitation had been issued and an appropriation of $200,000 made by Congress on the recommendation of Commander Folger, chief of ordnance, after he had seen a trial trip on Lake Michigan of an underwater boat invented by Mr. George C. Baker. This was an egg-shaped craft, propelled by a steam engine on the surface and storage-batteries when submerged, and controlled by two adjustable propellers, mounted on either side of the boat on a shaft running athwartship. These screws could be turned in any direction, so as to push or pull the vessel forward, downward, or at any desired angle. Mr. Baker submitted designs for a larger boat of the same kind, but they were not accepted.

The third inventor who entered the 1893 competition was Mr. Simon Lake, then a resident of Baltimore. He sent in the plans of the most astonishing-looking craft that had startled the eyes of the navy department since Ericsson's original monitor. It had two cigar-shaped hulls, one inside the other, the space between being used for ballast-tanks. It had no less than five propellors:

twin screws aft for propulsion, a single screw working in an open transverse tunnel forward,[1] to "swing the vessel at rest to facilitate pointing her torpedos," and two downhaul or vertical-acting propellers "for holding vessel to depth when not under way." These were not placed on deck, as on the *Nordenfeldt II*, but in slots in the keel. Other features of the bottom were two anchor

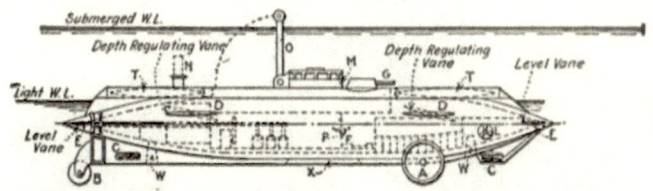

Courtesy International Marine Engineering.

Lake 1893 Design as Submitted to the U. S. Navy Department.

weights, a detachable "emergency keel," and a diving compartment. On deck were a folding periscope and a "gun arranged in watertight, revolving turret for defense purposes or attack on unarmored surface craft." There were four torpedo tubes, two forward and two aft, according to the modern German practice. The motive power was the then usual combination of steam and storage batteries. But the two remaining features of the 1893 model Lake submarine were extremely unusual.

Instead of one pair of horizontal rudders, there were four pairs, two large and two small. The latter, placed near the bow and stern, were "levelling vanes, designed automatically to hold the vessel on a level keel when under

[1] Mr. J. F. Waddington used vertical propellers in tubes through the vessel for keeping her on an even keel or submerging when stationary, on a small electric submarine he invented, built and demonstrated at Liverpool in 1886.

84   The Story of the Submarine

way"; while the larger ones were called "hydroplanes" and so located and designed as to steer the submarine under, not by making it dive bow foremost but by caus-

Courtesy of Mr. Simon Lake.

The *Argonaut Junior.*

ing it to submerge on an even keel. How this was to be accomplished will be explained presently. The other new thing about the Lake boat was that it was mounted on wheels for running along the sea-bottom. There were three of these wheels: a large pair forward on a strong axle for bearing the vessel's weight, and a small steering-wheel on the bottom of the rudder.

This submarine was never built, however, for the congressional appropriation was awarded to the Holland Torpedo-boat Company and Mr. Lake had at that time no means for building so elaborate a vessel by himself. What he did build was the simplest and crudest little submarine imaginable: the *Argonaut Jr.* She was a triangular box of yellow pine, fourteen feet long and five feet deep, mounted on three solid wooden wheels. She was trundled along the bottom of Sandy Hook Bay by one or two men cranking the axle of the two driving wheels. The boat was provided with an air-lock and diver's compartment "so arranged that by putting an air pressure on the diver's compartment equal to the water pressure outside, a bottom door could be opened and no water would come into the vessel. Then by putting on a pair of rubber boots the operator could walk around on the sea bottom and push the boat along with him and pick up objects, such as clams, oysters, etc., from the sea bottom." [2]

Enough people were convinced by the performances of this simple craft of the soundness of Mr. Lake's theories that the inventor was able to raise sufficient capital to build a larger submarine. This boat, which was designed in 1895 and built at Baltimore in 1897, was called the *Argonaut*. When launched, she had a cigar-shaped hull thirty-six feet long by nine in diameter, mounted on a pair of large toothed driving-wheels forward and a guiding-wheel on the rudder. The driving-wheels could

---

[2] Quotations in this chapter are from Mr. Lake's articles published in "International Marine Engineering," and are here reprinted by his kind permission.

be disconnected and left to revolve freely while the boat was driven by its single-screw propeller. There was a diver's compartment in the bottom and a "lookout compartment in the extreme bow, with a powerful searchlight to light up a pathway in front of her as she moved along over the waterbed. The searchlight I later found of little value except for night work in clear water. In clear water the sunlight would permit of as good vision without the use of the light as with it, while if the water was not clear, no amount of light would permit of vision through it for any considerable distance."

Storage batteries were carried only for working the searchlight and illuminating the interior of the boat. The *Argonaut* was propelled, both above and below the surface, by a thirty horse-power gasoline engine, the first one to be installed in a submarine. There was enough air to run it on, even when submerged, because the *Argonaut* was ventilated through a hose running to a float on the surface: a device later changed to two pipe masts long enough to let her run along the bottom at a depth of fifty feet.

The *Argonaut* had no hydroplanes or horizontal rudders of any kind. She was submerged, like the *Intelligent Whale*, by "two anchor weights, each weighing 1000 pounds, attached to cables, and capable of being hauled up or lowered by a drum and mechanism within the boat. . . . When it is desired to submerge the vessel the anchor weights are first lowered to the bottom; water is then allowed to enter the water-ballast compartments until her buoyancy is less than the weight of the two anchors, say 1500 pounds; the cables connecting with the weights are then hauled in, and the vessel is thus hauled to the bottom, until she comes to rest on her three wheels. The weights are then hauled into their pockets in the keel, and it is evident that she is resting on the wheels with a weight equal to the difference between her buoyancy with the weights at the bottom, and the weights in their pockets, or 500 pounds Now this weight may be increased or diminished, either by admitting more water into the bal-

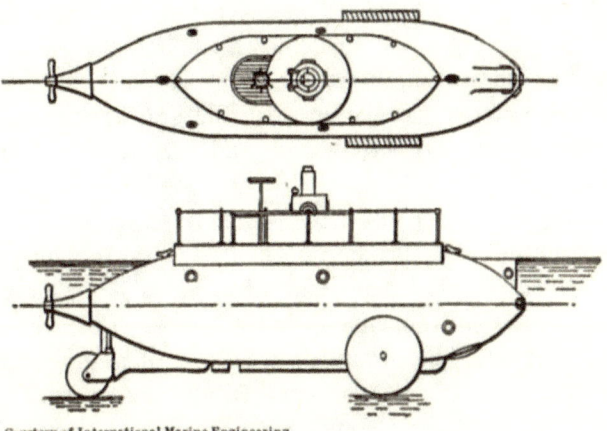

Argonaut as Originally Built.

last tanks or by pumping some out. Thus it will be seen that we have perfect control of the vessel in submerging her, as we may haul her down as fast or as slow as we please, and by having her rest on the bottom with sufficient weight to prevent the currents from moving her out of her course we may start up our propeller or driving-wheels and drive her at will over the bottom, the same as a tricycle is propelled on the surface of the earth in the upper air.

In muddy bottoms, we rest with a weight not much over 100 pounds; while on hard bottoms, or where there are strong currents, we sometimes rest on the bottom with a weight of from 1000 to 1500 pounds. . . .

"In the rivers we invariably found a muddy bed; in Chesapeake Bay we found bottoms of various kinds, in some places so soft that our divers would sink up to their knees, while in other places the ground would be hard, and at one place we ran across a bottom which was composed of a loose gravel, resembling shelled corn. Out in the ocean, however, was found the ideal submarine course, consisting of a fine gray sand, almost as hard as a macadamized road, and very level and uniform."

During this cruise under the waters of Chesapeake Bay, the *Argonaut* came on the wrecks of several sunken vessels, which Mr. Lake or some member of his crew examined through the open door in the bottom of the diving-compartment. The air inside was kept at a sufficiently high pressure to keep the water from entering, and the man in the submarine could pull up pieces of the wreck with a short boathook, or even reach down and place his bare hand on the back of a big fish swimming past. Sometimes members of the crew would put on diving-suits and walk out over the bottom, keeping in communication with the boat by telephone. Telephone stations were even established on the bottom of the bay, with cables running to the nearest exchange on shore, and conversations were held with people in Baltimore, Washington, and New York. (Perhaps the commanders of German submarines in British waters to-day are using this method to com-

The Lake Submarines

municate with German spies in London, Dublin, and Liverpool.)

The Spanish-American War was being fought while Mr. Lake was making these experiments. The entrance to Hampton Roads was planted with electric mines, but though he was forbidden to go too near them, the inventor proved that nothing would be easier than to locate the cable connecting them with the shore, haul it up into the diver's compartment of the *Argonaut* and cut it. He did this with a dummy cable of his own, and then repeatedly begged the navy department to let him take the *Argonaut* into the harbor of Santiago de Cuba and disable the mines that were keeping Admiral Sampson's fleet from going in and smashing the Spanish squadron there. But his offer, like that of John P. Holland, was refused.

"In 1898, also," says Mr. Lake, "the *Argonaut* made the trip from Norfolk to New York under her own power and unescorted. In her original form she was a cigar-shaped craft with only a small percentage of reserve buoyancy in her surface cruising condition. We were caught out in the severe November northeast storm of 1898 in which over two hundred vessels were lost and we did not succeed in reaching a harbor in the 'horseshoe' back of Sandy Hook until three o'clock in the morning. The seas were so rough they would break over her conning-tower in such masses I was obliged to lash myself fast to prevent being swept overboard. It was freezing weather and I was soaked and covered with ice on reaching harbor."

Mr. Lake then sent the *Argonaut* to a Brooklyn shipyard, where her original cigar-shaped hull was cut in half, and lengthened twenty feet, after which a light ship-shaped superstructure was built over her low sloping topsides. To keep it from being crushed in by water pressure when submerged, scupper-like openings were cut in the thin plating where it joined the stout, pressure-resisting hull, so that the superstructure automatically filled itself with sea-water on submerging and drained itself on rising again. Though uninhabitable, its interior supplied useful storage space, particularly for the gasoline fuel tanks, which, as Mr. Lake had already discovered, gave

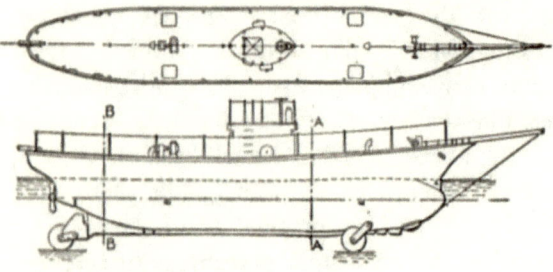

Courtesy of International Marine Engineering.
Argonaut as Rebuilt.

off fumes that soon rendered the air inside the submarine unbreathable, unless the tanks were kept outside instead of inside the hull. The swan-bow and long bowsprit of the new superstructure, together with the two ventilator-masts, gave the rebuilt *Argonaut* a schooner-like appearance, and her bowsprit has been compared to the whip-socket on the dashboard of the earliest automobiles. But Mr. Lake declares that this was no useless leftover but a practicable spring-buffer to guard against running into submerged rocks, while the bobstay helped the *Ar-*

gonaut to climb over the obstruction, as she could over anything on the sea-bottom she could get her bows over.

Primarily, the superstructure served to make the submarine more seaworthy as a surface-craft. Until then, most inventors and designers of undersea boats had confined their attentions to the problems of underwater navigation only, because, as had been pointed out by the monk Mersenne before 1648, even during the most violent storms the disturbance is felt but a little distance below the surface. But Mr. Lake realized that a submarine, like every other kind of boat, spends most of its existence on top of the water and that it is not always desirable to submerge whenever a moderate-sized wave sweeps over one of the old-fashioned, low-lying, cigar-shaped vessels. With her new superstructure, the *Argonaut* rode the waves as lightly as any yacht and ushered in the era of the sea-going submarine.

It was not until a year later that the *Narval,* a large double-hulled submarine with a ship-shaped outer shell of light, perforated plating, was launched in France. She was propelled by steam on the surface and by storage batteries when submerged. To distinguish this sea-going torpedo-boat, that could be submerged, from the earlier and simpler submarines designed and engined for underwater work only, her designer, M. Labeuf, called the *Narval* a "submersible." As the old type of boat soon became extinct, the distinction was not necessary and the old name "submarine" is still applied to all underwater craft. That Simon Lake and not M. Labeuf first gave the modern sea-going submarine its characteristic and essential superstructure is easily proved by dates. The

Narval was launched in October, 1899, the *Argonaut* was remodeled in December, 1898, and on April 2, 1897, Mr. Lake applied for and was presently granted the pioneer patent on a "combined surface and submarine vessel," the space between its cylindrical hull and the superstructure "being adapted to be filled with water when the vessel is submerged and thus rendered capable of resisting the pressure of the water."

But though in her remodeled form she became the forerunner of the long grim submarine cruisers of to-day, the *Argonaut* herself had been built to serve not as a warship but as a commercial vessel. Like her namesakes who followed Jason in the *Argo* to far-off Colchis for the Golden Fleece, she was to go forth in search of hidden treasure. She was to have been the first of a fleet of wheeled bottom-workers, salvaging the cargoes of wrecked ships; from the mail-bags of the latest lost liner to ingots and pieces-of-eight from the sand-clogged hulks of long-sunk Spanish galleons, or bringing up sponges, coral, and pearls from the depths of the tropic seas. But though he investigated a few wrecks and ingeniously transferred a few tons of coal from one into a submarine lighter by means of a pipe-line and a powerful force-pump, Mr. Lake has done nothing more to develop the fascinating commercial possibilities of the submarine since 1901, because he has been kept too busy building undersea warships for the United States and other naval powers.

Mr. Lake declares that one of his up-to-date wheeled submarines could enter a harbor-mouth defended by booms and nettings that would keep out either surface

Courtesy of International Marine Engineering.

The Rebuilt *Argonaut*, Showing Pipe-masts and Ship-shaped Superstructure.

torpedo boats or ordinary submarines. The smooth-backed bottom-worker of this special type would slip under the netting like a cat under a bead portière. If the netting were fastened down, a diver would step out through the door in the bottom of the submarine and either cut the netting from its moorings or attach a bomb

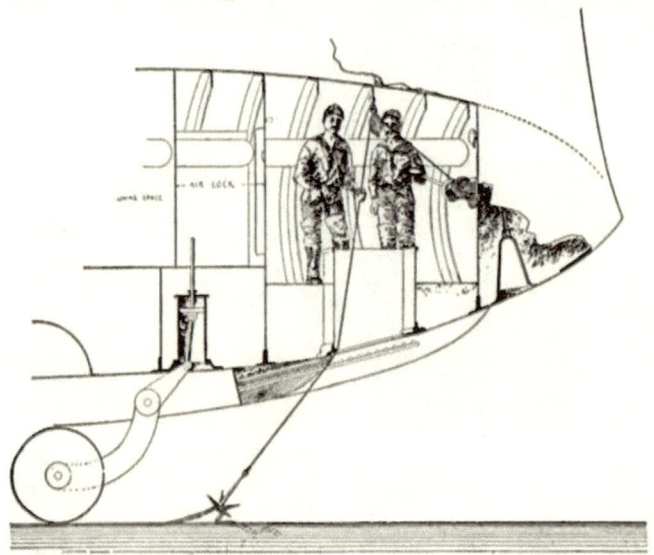

Courtesy of Mr. Simon Lake.
Cross-section of Diving-compartment on a Lake Submarine.

to blow a hole for the bottom-worker to go in through. An ordinary submarine, entering a hostile harbor, would be in constant danger of running aground in shallow water and either sticking there or rebounding to the surface, to be seen and fired at by the enemy. Even if its commander succeeded in keeping to the deep channel by dead reckoning — a process akin to flying blindfolded in an aeroplane up a crooked ravine and remembering just when and where to turn — even if he dodged the rocks and sand bars, he would be liable to bump the nose of his boat against an anchored contact mine(see Chapter XI). But the Lake bottom-worker would trundle steadily along, sampling the bottom to find where it was, and passing safely under the mines floating far above it. The divers would make short work of cutting the mine cables, or they might plant mines of their own under the ships in the harbor and blow them up as Bushnell tried to. Using electric motors and storage air-flasks, with no pipe masts or other "surface-indications" to betray its presence, one of these boats could remain snugly hid at the bottom of an enemy's harbor as long as its supplies held out.

As yet, however, we have not heard of any such exploits in the present war, though they seem perfectly feasible. Mr. Lake sold a boat designed for this sort of work and called the *Protector* to Russia in 1906.

The most characteristic feature of the Lake submarines is not the wheels, which are found only on those specially designed for bottom working, but the hydroplanes. These are horizontal rudders that are so placed and designed as to steer the boat forward and downward, but at the same time keeping it on an even keel. Bushnell and Nordenfeldt forced their boats straight up and down like buckets in a well, John P. Holland made his tip up its tail and dive like a loon, but Mr. Lake conceived the idea of having his boat descend like a suitcase carried by a man walking down-stairs: the suitcase moves steadily forward and downward towards the front door but it remains level. The first method with its vertical propellers wasted too much energy, the second incurred the risk of diving too fast and too deep, no matter whether the single pair of horizontal rudders were placed on the bow, or amidships, or on the stern. So Mr. Lake used two pairs of horizontal rudders "located at equal distances forward and aft of the center of gravity and buoyancy of the vessel when in the submerged condition, so as not to disturb the trim of the vessel when the planes were inclined down or up to cause the vessel to submerge or rise when under way." These he called hydroplanes, to distinguish them from another set of smaller horizontal rudders, which at first he called "leveling-vanes" and which were not used to steer the submarine under but manipulated to keep her at a constant depth and on a level keel while running submerged.

In theory, the early Lake boats were submerged on an even keel; in practice, they went under at an angle of several degrees. But they made nothing like the abrupt dives of the *Holland*.

"As the Electric Boat Company's boats (Holland type) increased in size," declares Chief Constructor D. W. Taylor, U.S.N., " bow rudders were fitted, and nowadays all submarines of this type in our navy are fitted with bow rudders as well as stern rudders. The Lake type submarines are still fitted with hydroplanes. But as you may see, means for effecting submergence have approached each other very closely: in fact, speaking generally, submarines all over the world now have two or more sets of diving-rudders; the most general arrangement is one pair forward and one pair aft; in some types three pairs are fitted, but this arrangement is more unusual.

"In general it may be said then that modern submarines of both types submerge in practically the same way. They assume a very slight angle of inclination, say a degree and a half or two degrees, and submerge at this angle. This may be said to be practically on an even keel."

Courtesy of International Marine Engineering.

Cross-section of the *Protector,* showing wheels stowed away when not running on the sea bottom.

The credit of originating this now world-wide practice of "level-keel submergence" obviously belongs, as "Who's Who in America" gives it, to

"Lake, Simon, naval architect, mechanical engineer. Born at Pleasantville, New Jersey, September 4, 1866; son of John Christopher and Miriam M. (Adams) Lake; educated at Clinton Liberal Institute, Fort Plain, New York, and Franklin Institute, Philadelphia; married Margaret Vogel of Baltimore, June 9, 1890. Inventor of even keel type of submarine torpedo boats; built first experimental boat, 1894; built *Argonaut*, 1897 (first submarine to operate successfully in the open sea); has designed and built many submarine torpedo boats for the United States and foreign countries; spent several years

Mr. Simon Lake.

in Russia, Germany, and England, designing, building, and acting in an advisory capacity in construction of submarine boats. Also inventor of submarine apparatus for locating and recovering sunken vessels and their cargoes; submarine apparatus for pearl and sponge fishing, heavy

The Lake Submarines

oil internal combustion engine for marine propulsion, etc. Member of the Society of Naval Architects and Marine Engineers, American Society of Mechanical Engineers, American Society of Naval Engineers, Institute of Naval Architects (London), Schffsbautechnische Gesellschaft (Berlin). Mason. *Clubs,* Engineers' (New York), Algonquin, (Bridgeport, Connecticut). *Home,* Milford, Connecticut. *Office,* Bridgeport, Connecticut."

When the Krupps first took up the idea of constructing submarines for the German and Russian governments, the great German firm consulted with Mr. Lake, who was at that time living in Europe. An elaborate contract was drawn up between them. The Krupps agreed to employ Mr. Lake in an advisory capacity and to build " Lake type " boats, both in Russia, where they were to erect a factory and share the profits with him, and in Germany, on a royalty basis. Before he could sign this contract, Mr. Lake had to obtain the permission of the directors of his own company in Bridgeport. In the meanwhile, he gave the German company his most secret plans and specifications. But the Krupps never signed the contract, withdrew from going into Russia, and their lawyer coolly told Mr. Lake that, as he had failed to patent his inventions in Germany, his clients were perfectly free to build " Lake type " submarines there without paying him anything and were going to do so.

The famous Krupp-built German submarines that are playing so prominent a part in the present war are therefore partly of American design. Whenever Mr. Lake reads that another one of them has been destroyed by the Allies, his emotions must be rather mixed.

CHAPTER IX

A TRIP IN A MODERN SUBMARINE

LIEUTENANT PERRY SCOPE, commanding the X-class flotilla, was sitting in his comfortable little office on the mother-ship *Ozark*, when I entered with a letter from the secretary of the navy, giving me permission to go on board a United States submarine. Without such authorization no civilian may set foot on the narrow decks of our undersea destroyers, though he may visit a battleship with no more formality than walking into a public park.

"We're too small and full of machinery to hold a crowd," explained the lieutenant, "and the crowd wouldn't enjoy it if they came. No nice white decks for the girls to dance on or fourteen-inch guns for them to sit on while they have their pictures taken. Besides, everything's oily — you'd better put on a suit of overalls instead of those white flannels."

There were plenty of spare overalls on the *Ozark*, for she was the mother-ship of a family of six young submarines. Built as a coast defense monitor shortly after the Spanish War, she had long since been retired from the fighting-line, and was now the floating headquarters, dormitory, hospital, machine-shop, bakery, and general store for the six officers and the hundred and fifty men of the flotilla.

Photo by Brown Bros.

U. S. Submarine E-2.

Note wireless, navigating-bridge, and openings for flooding superstructure when submerging.

Moored alongside the parent-ship, the submarine *X-4* was filling her fuel-tanks with oil through a pipe-line, in preparation for the day's cruise and target-practice I was to be lucky enough to witness. Two hundred and fifty feet long, flat-decked and straight-stemmed, she looked, except for the lack of funnels, much more like a surface-going torpedo-boat than the landsman's conventional idea of a submarine.

"I thought she would be cigar-shaped," I said as we went on board.

"She is — underneath," answered Lieutenant Scope. "What you see is only a light-weight superstructure or false hull built over the real one. See those holes in it, just above the water line? They are to flood the superstructure with whenever we submerge, otherwise the water pressure would crush in these thin steel plates like veneering. But it makes us much more seaworthy for surface work, gives us a certain amount of deckroom, and stowage-space for various useful articles, such as this."

Part of the deck rose straight up into the air, like the top of a freight-elevator coming up through the sidewalk. Beneath the canopy thus formed was a short-barreled, three-inch gun.

"Fires a twelve-pound shell, like the field-pieces the landing-parties take ashore from the battleships," explained the naval officer, as he trained the vicious-looking little cannon all around the compass. "Small enough to be handy, big enough to sink any merchant ship afloat, or smash anything that flies."

A Trip in a Modern Submarine   103

Here he pointed the muzzle straight up as if gunning for hostile aeroplanes.

"And please observe," he concluded, as the gun sank down into its lair again, "how that armored hatch-cover protects the gun-crew from shrapnel or falling bombs."

I followed him to the conning-tower, or, as he always spoke of it, the turret. The little round bandbox of the *Holland* has developed into a tall, tapering structure, sharply pointed fore and aft to lessen resistance when running submerged. Above the turret was a small navigating-bridge, screened and roofed with canvas, where a red-haired quartermaster stood by the steering-wheel, and saluted as we came up the ladder. The lieutenant put the engine-room telegraph over to "Start," and a mighty motor throbbed underneath our feet. Then the mooring was cast off, the telegraph put over to "Slow Ahead," and the *X-4* put out to sea.

"How long a cruise could she make?" I asked.

"Four thousand miles is her radius," answered her commander. "Back in 1915, ten American-designed submarines crossed from Canada to England under their own power."

"Yet it is only a few years since we were told that submarines could only be used for coast defense, unless they were carried inside their mother-ships and launched near the scene of battle," I remarked. "Or that each battleship should carry a dinky little submarine on deck and lower it over the side like a steam-launch."

"People said the same thing about torpedo-boats,"

agreed the lieutenant; "they began as launches — now look at the size of that destroyer smoking along over there. Ericsson thought that any ironclad bigger than a Civil War monitor would be an unwieldy monster. Even John P. Holland fought tooth and nail against increasing the length of his submarines. This boat of mine is five times the length of the old *Holland*, but she's only a primitive ancestor of the perfect submarine of the future."

"She isn't a submarine at all," I replied presently, as the *X-4* swept on down the coast at a good twenty-two knots, her foredeck buried in foam and the sea-breeze singing through the antennæ of her wireless. "She's nothing but a big motor-boat."

"And she's got some big motors," replied the lieutenant. "Better step below and have a look at them."

I went down through the open hatchway to the interior of the boat and aft to the engine-room. There I found two long, many-cylindered oil-engines of strange design, presided over by a big blond engineer whose grease-spotted dungarees gave no hint as to his rating.

"What kind of machines are these?" I shouted above the roar they made. "And why do you need two of them?"

"Diesel heavy-oil engines," he answered. "One for each propeller."

"What is the difference between one of these and the gasoline engine of a motor-car? I know a little about that."

"Do you know what the carburetor is?" asked the engineer.

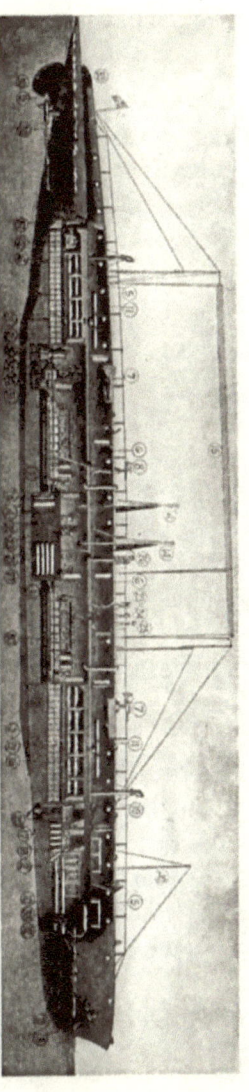

Courtesy of International Marine Engineering.

A Submarine Cruiser, or Fleet Submarine (Lake Type).

The parts indicated by numbers in this illustration are as follows: 1, main ballast tanks; 2, fuel tanks; 3, keel; 4, safety drop keel; 5, habitable superstructure; 6, escape and safety chambers; 7, disappearing anti-air craft guns; 8, rapid fire gun; 9, torpedo tubes; 10, twin deck torpedo tubes; 11, torpedo firing tank; 13, anchor; 14, periscopes; 15, wireless; 16, crew's quarters; 17, officers' quarters; 18, war head stowage; 19, torpedo hatch; 20, diving chamber; 21, electric storage battery; 22, galley; 23, steering gear; 24, binnacle; 25, searchlight; 26, conning tower; 27, diving station; 28, control tank; 29, compressed air flasks; 30, forward engine room and engines; 31, after engine room and engines; 32, central control compartment; 33, torpedo room; 34, electric motor room; 35, switchboard; 36, ballast pump; 37, auxiliary machinery room; 38, hydroplane; 39, vertical rudders; 40, signal masts.

"That's where the gasoline is mixed with air, before it goes into the cylinder."

The engineer nodded.

"The mixture is sucked into the cylinder by the down-stroke of the piston. The up-stroke compresses it, and then the mixture is exploded by an electric spark from the spark-plug. The force of the explosion drives the piston down, and the next stroke up drives out the refuse gases. That's how an ordinary, four-cycle gasoline motor works.

"But the Diesel engine," he continued, "doesn't need any carburetor or spark-plug. When the piston makes its first upward or compression-stroke, there is nothing in the cylinder but pure air. This is compressed to a pressure of about 500 pounds a square inch — and when you squeeze anything as hard as that, you make it mighty hot —"

"Like a blacksmith pounding a piece of cold iron to a red heat?" I suggested. The engineer nodded again.

"That compressed air is so hot that the oil which has been spurted in through an injection-valve is exploded, and drives the piston down on the power-stroke. The waste gases are then blown out by compressed air. There are an air-compressor and a storage tank just for scavenging, or blowing the waste gases out of every three power-cylinders."

"What are the advantages of the Diesel over the gasoline engine?"

"In the first place, it gives more power. You see, three out of every four strokes made by the piston of a gasoline engine — suction-stroke, compression-stroke, and scavenging-stroke — waste power instead of producing it. But the Diesel is what we call a two-cycle engine; its piston makes only two trips for each power-stroke. In the second place, it is cheaper, because instead of gasoline it uses heavy, low-price oil. And this makes it much safer, for the heavy oil does not vaporize so easily. The

Courtesy of the Electric Boat Company.
Auxiliary Switchboard and Electric Cook-stove, in a U. S. Submarine.

air in some of the old submarines that used gasoline motors would get so that it was like trying to breathe inside a carburetor, and there was always the chance of a spark from the electric motors exploding the whole business, and your waking up to find the trained nurse changing your bandages. The German navy refused to build a submarine as long as there was nothing better than gasoline to propel it on the surface. They did n't launch their *U-1* till 1906, after Dr. Diesel had got his motor into practicable shape. It cost him twenty years of hard work, but without his motor we could n't have the modern submarine. And they 're using it more and more in ocean freighters. There's a line of motor-ships running to-day between Scandinavia and San Francisco, through the Panama Canal.

"Aft of the Diesel, here," continued the engineer, " is our electric motor, for propelling her when submerged. Reverse it and have it driven by the Diesel engine, and the motor serves as a dynamo to generate electricity for charging the batteries. As long as we can get oil and come to the surface to use it, we can never run short of ' juice.' [1]

"Besides turning the propeller, the electricity from the batteries lights the boat, and turns the ventilating fans, works the air-compressor for the torpedo-tubes, drives all the big and little pumps, runs a lot of auxiliary motors that haul up the anchor, turn the rudders, and do other odd jobs, it heats the boat in cold weather —"

"And cooks the grub all the year round, don't forget that, Joe," said another member of the crew. "Luncheon is served in the palm room."

We ate from a swinging table let down from the ceiling of the main- or living-compartment of the submarine, that extended forward from the engine-room to the tiny officers' cabin and the torpedo room in the bows. Tiers of canvas bunks folded up against the walls showed where the crew slept when on a cruise. For lunch that day we had bread baked on the mother-ship, butter out of a can, fried ham, fried potatoes, and coffee hot from a little

[1] Electric current.

electric stove such as you can see in the kitchenette of a light-housekeeping apartment on shore. The lieutenant's lunch was carried up to him on the bridge. When the meal was over, most of the men went on deck, and my friend the engineer put a large cigar in his mouth. I

Courtesy of the Electric Boat Company.
Forward deck of a U. S. Submarine, in cruising trim.

took out a box of matches and was about to strike one for his benefit when he stopped me, saying,

"Don't ever strike a light in a submarine or a dynamite factory. It's unhealthy."

I apologized profusely.

"The air is so much better than I had expected that I forgot where I was."

"Yes," said the engineer, chewing his unlighted cigar, "there is plenty of good air in a big modern boat like this, running on the surface in calm weather and with the main hatch and all ventilators open. But come with us when we're bucking high seas or running submerged on a breathing-diet of canned air flavored with oil, and you'll understand why so many good men have been invalided out of the flotilla with lung-trouble. We're the only warships without any dogs or parrots or other mascots on board, for no animal could endure the air in a submarine."

Courtesy of the Electric Boat Company.
Same, preparing to submerge. Railing stowed away and bow-rudders extended.

"I thought every submarine carried a cage of white mice, because they began to squeak as soon as the air began to get bad and so warned the crew."

"That was a crude device of the early days," replied the engineer. "We don't carry white mice any more, though I believe they still use them in the British navy."

I went up on deck, to find that the *X-4* had reached the practice-grounds and was being made ready for a

A Trip in a Modern Submarine

dive. Her crew were busy dismantling and stowing away the bridge and the light deck-railing, hauling down the flag, and closing all ventilators and other openings.

"How long has it taken you to get ready?" I asked Lieutenant Scope.

"Twenty minutes," he answered. "But the real diving takes only two minutes. We'll go below now, sink her to condition, and run her under with the diving rudders."

"What are those things unfolding themselves on either side of the bows?" I asked. "I thought the diving rudders were carried astern."

"Modern submarines are so long that they need them both fore and aft," replied the lieutenant. "As you see, the diving rudders fold flat against the side of the boat where they will be out of harm's way when we are running on the surface or lying alongside the mother-ship. Better come below now, for we're going to dive."

We descended into the turret and the hatch was closed. The Diesel engines had already been stopped and the electric motors were now turning the propellers.

"Why are those big electric pumps working down there?" I asked.

"Pumping water into the ballast-tanks."

"But doesn't the water run into the tanks anyhow, as soon as you open the valves?" I asked the lieutenant.

"Turn a tumbler upside down and force it down into a basin of water," he replied, "and you trap some air in the top of the tumbler, which prevents the water from rising beyond a certain point. The same thing takes place in our tanks, and to fill them we have to force in the water with powerful pumps that compress the air in the tanks to a very small part of its original bulk. This compressed air acts as a powerful spring to drive the water out of the tanks again when we wish to rise. By blowing out the tanks, a submarine can come to the surface in twenty seconds or one sixth the time it takes to submerge."

"When are we going under?" I asked him. The lieutenant looked at his watch and answered,

"We have been submerged for the last four minutes."

I experienced a feeling of the most profound disappointment. Ever since I had been a very small boy I had been looking forward to the time when I should go down in a submarine boat, and now that time had passed without my realizing it.

"But why did n't I feel the boat tilt when she dived?" I demanded.

"Because she went down a very gentle slope, between two and three degrees at the steepest. The only way you could have noticed it would have been to watch these gages."

Large dials on the wall of the turret indicated that the X-4 was running on what was practically an even keel at a depth of sixteen feet and under a consequent water-pressure of 1024 pounds on every square foot of her hull.

"How deep could she go?"

"One hundred and fifty feet — if she had to. The strong inner hull of a modern submarine is built up of three quarter inch plates of the best mild steel and well braced and strengthened from within. But as a rule there is no need of our diving below sixty feet at the deepest, or far enough to clear the keel of the largest ship. You will notice how the depth-control man is holding her steady by manipulating the forward horizontal rudders, just as an aviator steadies his aeroplane."

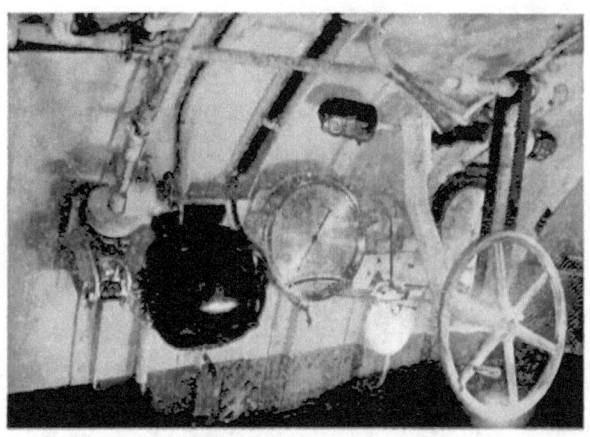

Courtesy of the Electric Boat Company.
Depth-control Station, U. S. Submarine.
Wheel governing horizontal rudders, gages showing depth, trim, etc.

"He must be a strong man to handle those two big horizontal rudders."

"He has an electric motor to do the hard work for him, as has the quartermaster steering the course here with the vertical rudder."

The same red-headed petty officer that I had noticed on the bridge now grasped the spokes of a smaller steering-wheel inside the conning-tower.

"What is that queer-looking thing whirling round and round in front of him?" I asked.

"A Sperry gyroscopic compass," replied the lieutenant.

"An ordinary magnetic compass could not be relied on to point in any particular direction if it was shut up in a steel box full of charged electric wires, like the turret of a submarine. We tried to remedy this by building conning-towers of copper, till Mr. Sperry perfected a compass that has no magnetic needle, but operates on the principle of the gyroscope. You know that a heavy, rapidly rotating wheel resists any tendency to being shifted relative to space?"

"Yes."

"The earth, revolving on its axis, is nothing but a big gyroscope — that is why it stays put. The little gyroscope on this compass spins at right angles to the revolution of the earth and so keeps in a due north and south line. But the frame it is mounted on turns with the ship, so the relative positions of the frame and the gyro-axis show in what direction the submarine is heading."

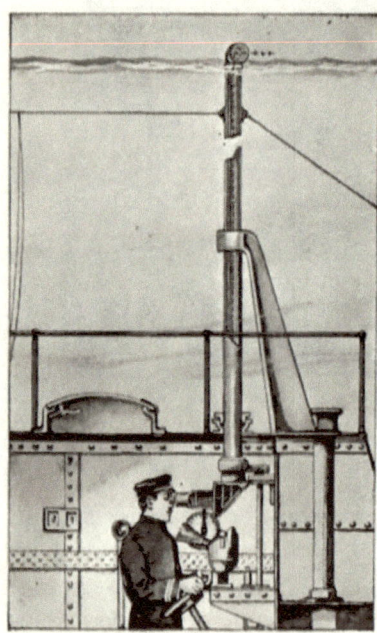

Cross-section of a Periscope.

"And you can see what's ahead of you through the periscope. Who invented that?"

"The idea is a very old one. Certain French and

Dutch inventors designed submarines with periscopes as long ago as the eighteen-fifties. In the Civil War, the light-draft river-monitor *Osage* had attached to her turret a crude periscope made by her chief engineer, Thomas Doughty, out of a piece of three-inch steam-pipe with holes cut at each of its ends at opposite sides, and pieces of looking-glass inserted as reflectors. By means of this instrument her captain, now Rear-Admiral, Thomas O. Selfridge, was able to look over the high banks of the Red River when the *Osage* had run aground in a bend and was being attacked by three thousand dismounted Confederate cavalry, who were repulsed with the loss of four hundred killed or wounded by the fire of the monitor's 11-inch guns, directed through the periscope.[2]

"But as late as 1900 the periscope was so crude and unsatisfactory an instrument that John P. Holland would have nothing to do with it. The credit for bringing it to its present efficiency belongs chiefly to the Germans, who kept many of their scientists working together on the solution of the difficult problems of optics that were involved.

"By turning this little crank," the lieutenant continued, "I can revolve the reflector at the top of the tube. This reflector contains a prism which reflects the image of the object in view down through a system of lenses in the tube to another prism here at the bottom, where the observer sees it through an eyepiece and telescope lenses."

I looked into the eyepiece, which was so much like that of an old-fashioned stereoscope that I felt that it, too, ought to work back and forth after the manner of a

[2] From an article by Admiral Selfridge in the "Outlook."

slide trombone. I found myself looking out over the broad blue waters of a sunlit bay. I noticed a squall blackening the surface of the water, a catboat running before it, and the gleam of the brass instruments of the band playing on the after deck of a big white excursion steamer half a mile away.

"I can almost imagine I can hear the music of that band," I exclaimed. "The optical illusion is perfect."

"It has to be," rejoined the lieutenant. "If the image were in the least distorted or out of perspective, we couldn't aim straight."

"What do you do when the periscope is wet with spray?" I asked him.

"Wash the glass with a jet of alcohol and dry it from the inside with a current of warm air passing up and down the tube. A periscope-tube is double: the outer one passing through a stuffing-box in the hull, and the inner tube revolving inside it. The old-fashioned single tubes were too hard to revolve and the resistance of the water used to bend them aft and cause leakage. We can raise and lower the periscopes at will, and all our larger boats have two of them, so that they can keep a lookout in two directions at once, besides having a spare eye in case the first is put out."

"What are those two little things that big naval tug is towing over there?" I inquired.

"The target for our torpedo practice," replied Lieutenant Scope. "We shall try to put four Whiteheads between those two buoys as the tug tows them past at an unknown range and speed. If you step forward to the torpedo room you can see them loading the tubes."

A Trip in a Modern Submarine 117

As I walked forward it occurred to me that the twenty-odd men on board the *X-4* seemed to be moving about inside her with perfect freedom, without disturbing her trim. I mentioned this to one of the crew.

"It's the trimming-tanks that keep her level," he explained. "As we're walking forward, our weight in water is being automatically pumped from the trimming-

Courtesy of the Electric Boat Company.

Forward torpedo-compartment, U. S. Submarine, showing breech-mechanism of four tubes. Round opening above is the escape-hatch.

tank in the bow to the one astern. A submarine is just one blamed tank after another. Stand clear of that chain-fall, sir; they're loading No. 1 tube."

Stripped to the waist like an old-time gun-crew, four beautifully muscled young gunner's mates were hoisting, with an ingenious arrangement of chains and pulleys, a torpedo from the magazine. The breach of the tube was opened and the long Whitehead thrust in, two flanges on its sides being fitted into deep grooves in the sides of the tube, so that the torpedo would not spin like a rifle-bullet but be launched on an even keel. The breach was closed, and the men stood by expectantly.

"Skipper's up in the conning-tower, taking aim through the periscope," explained the man who had told me about trimming-tanks. "The tubes being fixed in the bow, he has to train the whole boat like a gun. Likewise he's got to figure out how far it is to the target and how fast the tug is towing it, how many seconds it's going to take the torpedo to get there, and how much he's got to allow for its being carried off its course by tide and currents. When he gets good and ready, the lieutenant'll press a little electric button and you'll hear —"

"THUD!" went the compressed air in the tube, and the submarine shuddered slightly with the shock of the recoil. But that was all.

"There she goes!" said my friend the tank-expert. "As soon as the Whitehead was expelled, a compensation-tank just above the tube was flooded with enough water to make good the loss in weight."

"What keeps the sea-water from rushing into the tube after the torpedo leaves it?" I asked.

"A conical-shaped cap on the bow of the boat keeps both tubes closed except when you want to fire one of them. Then the cap, which is pivoted on its upper edge, swings to port or starboard just long enough for the torpedo to get clear and swings back before the water can get in."

Four of the ten torpedoes carried in the magazine were sped on their way to the unseen target. I returned to

A Trip in a Modern Submarine

the turret as the wireless operator entered and handed a typewritten slip to Lieutenant Scope, who smiled happily and said to me,

"The captain of the tug reports that all four shots were hits and all four torpedoes have been safely recovered."

I was too astonished to congratulate him on his marksmanship, as I should have done.

"How in the name of miracles!" I gasped. "Can you receive a wireless telegram under the sea?"

"By the Fessenden oscillator," he replied, and added to the wireless man,

"Take this gentleman below and show him how it works."

"Did you ever have another chap knock two stone together under water when you were taking a dive?" asked the operator. I nodded in vivid recollection.

"Then you have some idea how sounds are magnified under water. It is an old idea to put submarine bells down under lighthouses and fit ships with some kind of receiver so that the bells can be heard and warning given when it is too foggy to see the light. The advantage over the old-style bell-buoy lies in the fact that sound travels about four times as fast through water as through air,[3] and goes further and straighter because it isn't deflected by winds or what the aviators call 'air-pockets.' The man who knows most about these things is Professor Fessenden, of the Submarine Signal Company of Boston,

[3] The velocity of sound in dry air at a temperature of 32 degrees Fahrenheit is about 1087 feet a second, in water at 44 degrees, about 4708 feet a second.

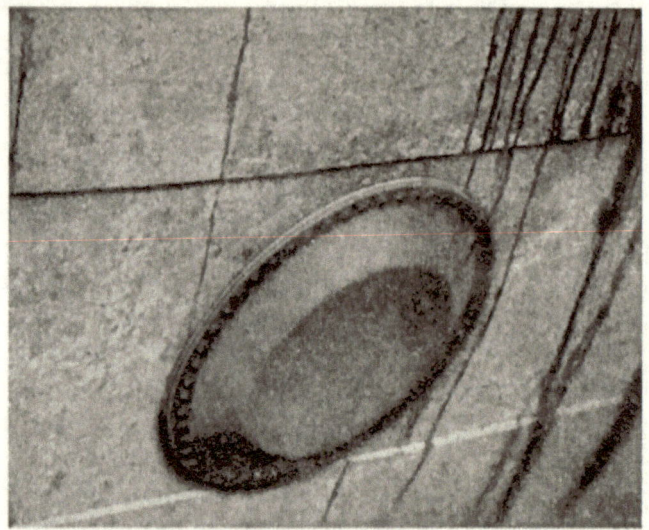

Courtesy of the American Magazine.

Fessenden oscillator outside the hull of a ship. The "ear" of a modern vessel.

who first realized the possibility of telegraphing through water.[4]

"Fastened outside the hull of this boat is one of the Fessenden oscillators: a steel disk eighteen inches in diameter, that can be vibrated very rapidly by electricity.

---

[4] The sound of the first gun of the salute fired by the Russian fleet in Cronstadt harbor to celebrate the coronation of Alexander II in 1855 was the signal for the crew of the submerged submarine *Le Diable Marin* to begin singing the National Anthem. Their voices, accompanied by a band of four pieces, were distinctly heard above the surface. This novel concert had been planned by Wilhelm Bauer, the designer of the submarine and one of the earliest students of under-water acoustics. He succeeded in signaling from one side of the harbor to another by striking a submerged piece of sheet-iron with a hammer.

A Trip in a Modern Submarine

These vibrations travel through the water, like wireless waves through the ether, till they strike the oscillator on another vessel and set it to vibrating in sympathy. To send a message, I start and stop the oscillator with this key so as to form the dots and dashes of the Morse code. To receive, I sit here with these receivers over my ears and 'listen in,' just like a wireless operator, till I pick up our call 'X-4,' 'X-4.'"

"How far can you send a message under water?"

"Ten miles is the furthest I've ever sent one. Professor Fessenden has sent messages more than thirty miles. The invention only dates back to 1913 and what it will do in the future, there is no telling."

"Even now, could n't a surface vessel act as eyes for

Courtesy of the American Magazine.

Professor Fessenden receiving a message sent through several miles of sea-water by his "Oscillator."

a whole flotilla of submarines and tell them where to go and when to strike by coaching them through the Fessenden oscillator?"

The operator nodded.

"We're doing it to-day, in practice. But don't forget that an enemy's ship carrying a pair of oscillators can hear a submarine coming two miles away. You can make out the beat of a propeller at that distance every time."

"But how can you tell how far away and in what direction it is?"

"I can't, with a single oscillator like ours. But a ship carries two of them, one on each side of the hull, like the ears on a man's head. And just as a man knows whether a shout he hears comes from the right or left, because he hears it more with one ear than the other, so the skipper of a surface craft can look at the indicator that registers the relative intensity of the vibrations received by the port and starboard oscillators and say,

"'There's somebody three points off the starboard bow, mile and three quarters away, and heading for us. Nothing in sight, so it must be one of those blamed submarines.'

"And away he steams, full speed ahead and cutting zigzags. Or maybe he gets his rapid-fire guns ready and watches for Mr. Submarine to rise — like the X-4's doing now."

Freed of the dead weight of many tons of sea water blown from her ballast-tanks by compressed air, the submarine rose to the surface like a balloon. Ventilators and hatch-covers were thrown open and we swarmed up on deck to fill our grateful lungs with the good sea air. Three motor-boats from the tug throbbed up alongside with the four torpedoes we had discharged.

"Those boats wait, one this side of the target, one near it and the third over on the far side, to mark the shots and catch the torpedoes after they rise to the surface at the end of their run," said Lieutenant Scope. "We very seldom lose a torpedo nowadays. They tell a story about one that dived to the bottom and was driven by the force of its own engines into forty feet of soft mud, where it stayed till it happened to be dug up by a dredger."

The four torpedoes were hoisted aboard, drained of the sea water that had flooded their air-chambers, cleaned and lowered through the torpedo hatch forward down into the magazine. By this time the bridge and railing were again in place and the flags fluttering over the taffrail as the *X-4*, her day's work done, sped swiftly up the coast to home and mother-ship.

CHAPTER X

ACCIDENTS AND SAFETY DEVICES

THE following submarines, with all or part of their crews, have been accidentally lost in time of peace:

Date	Name	Nationality	Men Lost
March 18, 1904	A-1	British	11
June 20, 1904	Delfin	Russian	26
June 8, 1905	A-8	British	14
July 6, 1905	Farfadet	French	14
October 16, 1906	Lutin	French	13
April 26, 1909	Foca	Italian	13
June 12, 1909	Kambala	Russian	20
July 14, 1909	C-11	British	13
April 15, 1910	No. 6.	Japanese	14
May 26, 1910	Pluviôse	French	26
January 17, 1911	U-3	German	3
February 2, 1912	A-3	British	14
June 8, 1912	Vendémiaire	French	24
October 4, 1912	B-2	British	15
June 8, 1913	E-5	British	3
December 10, 1913	C-14	British	none
January 16, 1914	A-7	British	11
March 25, 1915	F-4	American	21

The *A-1* was engaged in manœuvers off Spithead, England, when she rose to the surface right under the bows of the fast-steaming Union Castle Liner *Berwick Castle*. Before anything could be done, the sharp prow of the steamer had cut a great gash in the thin hull of the submarine and sent her to the bottom with all her crew. This was in broad daylight; her sister-ship *C-11* was

Accidents and Safety Devices 125

rammed and sunk by another liner three years later, at night. The *Pluviôse* of the French navy escaped the bow of an on-coming cross-channel steamer when the submarine came up at the entrance to Calais Harbor, only to have her topsides crushed in by a blow from one of the paddle-wheels. Collisions like these are less likely to happen nowadays, for the navigating officer of a modern submarine can take a look round the horizon through the periscope from a depth sufficient to let most steamers pass harmlessly over him, and in case of darkness or fog, he can detect the vibrations of approaching propellers by means of the Fessenden oscillator or some similar device. Yet the frequency with which submarines have been intentionally rammed and sunk in the present war shows that they would still be liable to rise blindly to their destruction in time of peace.

The vapor from a leaking fuel-tank, making an explosive mixture with the air inside the submarine and set off by a spark from the electrical machinery, has caused many accidents of another kind. Such an explosion took place on the original *Holland*, shortly after she was taken into the government service, but fortunately without killing any one. As the crew of the British *A-5* were filling the fuel tanks of their vessel with gasoline, some of them were blown up through the open hatchway and into the sea by a burst of flaming vapor that killed six men and terribly injured twelve more. A rescue party that entered the boat to save the men still left aboard had several of its own members disabled by a second explosion. The vessel itself, however, was almost unharmed. But not long afterwards, another submarine of the same ill-fated class, the *A-8*, was lying off Plymouth breakwater with her hatches open, when the people on shore heard three distinct explosions on board her and saw her suddenly submerge. Her crew evidently got the hatches closed before she went down, as they sent up signals that they were alive but unable to rise. Two hours later a fourth explosion took place and all hope was abandoned.

This danger has been guarded against by better construction of tanks and valves, and very greatly lessened by the substitution of the heavy oil used in the Diesel engines for the more costly and volatile gasoline.

Besides igniting explosive oil vapors with their sparks, the old-fashioned sulphuric acid and lead storage batteries still used in many submarines are a great source of danger in themselves. The jars are too easily broken, and the leaking acid eats into the steel plating of the boat, weakening it if not actually letting in the sea water. And if salt water comes in contact with a battery of this type, then chlorin gas — the same poisonous gas that the Germans use against the Allies' trenches — is generated and the crew are in very great danger of suffocation. The new Edison alkali storage battery, besides being lighter and more durable, uses no acid and cannot give off chlorin when saturated with sea water.

The remaining great danger is that a submarine may get out of control and submerge too quickly, so that it either strikes the bottom, at the risk of being crushed in or entangled, or descends to so great a depth that its sides are forced in by the pressure of the water outside, which also prevents the submarine from discharging the water in its ballast tanks and escaping to the surface.

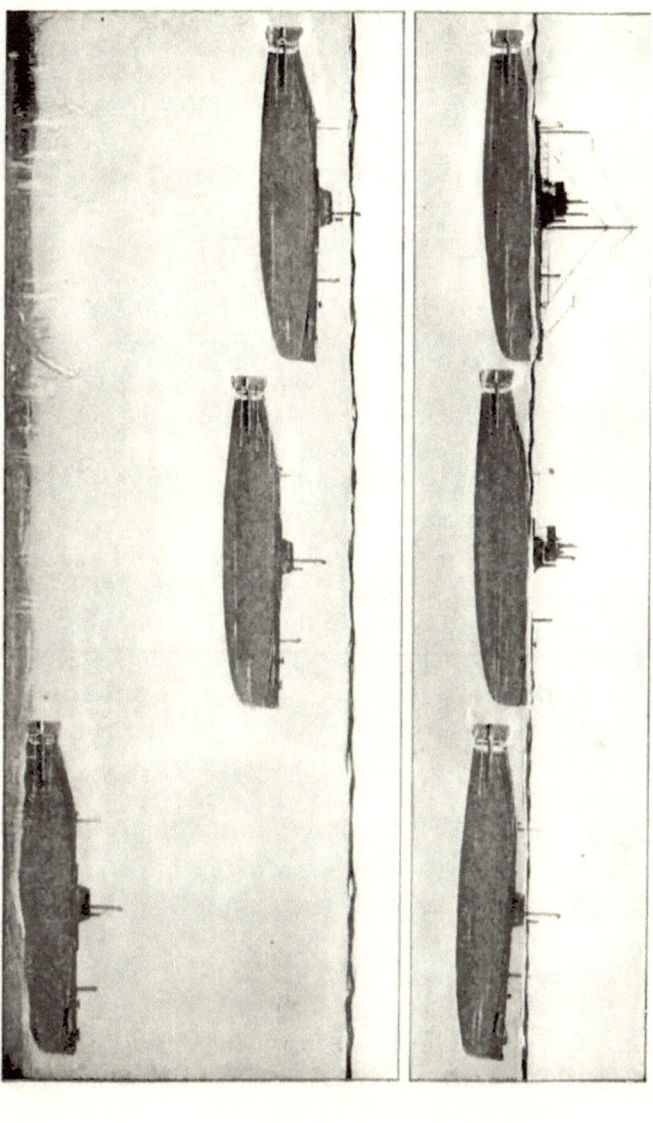

Side-elevation of a Modern Submarine.

A, Running on the surface; B, In awash condition; C, Submerging; D, Exposing periscope; E, Fully submerged; F, Resting on the bottom.

Redrawn from the London Sphere.

Detachable safety weights and keels to lighten the boat in such an emergency date back to the time of Bushnell and J. Day. A more modern device is to have a hydrostatic valve (see page 51) set to correspond with the pressure of a certain depth of water, so that if the submarine goes below this the valve will be forced in and automatically " blow the tanks."

A submarine that sank too deep was the *No. 6,* of the Imperial Japanese navy, which disappeared while manœuvering in Hiroshima Bay, on April 15, 1910. When she was found, her entire crew lay dead at their stations, and in the conning-tower, beside the body of the commander, was the following letter written by that officer, Lieutenant Takuma Faotomu:

"Although there is indeed no excuse to make for the sinking of his Imperial Majesty's boat, and for the doing away of subordinates through my heedlessness, all on board the boat have discharged their duties well and in everything acted calmly until death. Although we are dying in the pursuance of our duty to the State, the only regret we have is due to anxiety lest the men of the world misunderstand the matter, and that thereby a blow may be given to the future development of the submarine.

"Gentlemen, we hope you will be increasingly diligent and not fail to appreciate the cause of the accident, and that you will devote your entire energy to investigate everything and so secure the future development of submarines. If this be done we have nothing to regret.

"While going through gasoline submerged exercises we submerged too far, and when we attempted to shut the sluice-valve, the chain broke.

Accidents and Safety Devices

"Then we tried to close the sluice-valve by hand, but it was too late, for the afterpart was full of water, and the boat sank at an angle of about twenty-five degrees. The boat came to rest at an incline of about twelve degrees, pointing towards the stern. The switchboard being under water the electric lights went out. Offensive gas developed and breathing became difficult. The boat sank about 10 A.M. on the 15th, and though suffering at the time from this offensive gas, we endeavored to expel the water by hand pumps. As the vessel went down we expelled the water from the main tank. As the light has gone out the gage cannot be seen, but we know the water has been expelled from the main tank.

"We cannot use the electric current at all. The battery is leaking but no salt water has reached it and chlorin gas has not developed. We only rely on the hand pump now.

"The above was written under the light of the conning-tower, at about 11.45 o'clock. We are now soaked by the water that has made its way in. Our clothes are wet and we feel cold. I had been accustomed to warn my shipmates that their behavior (in an emergency) should be calm and deliberate, as well as brave, yet not too deliberate, lest work be retarded. People may be tempted to ridicule this after this failure, but I am perfectly confident that my words have not been mistaken.

"The depth gage of the conning-tower indicates 52 feet, and despite our efforts to expel the water the pump stopped and would not work after 12 o'clock. The depth in this neighborhood being ten fathoms, the reading may be correct.

"The officers and men of submarines should be chosen from the bravest of the brave or there will be annoyances in cases like this. Happily all the members of this crew have discharged their duties well and I am satisfied. I have always expected death whenever I left my home, and therefore my will is already in the drawer at Karasaki. (This remark applies only to my private affairs and is really superfluous. Messrs. Taguchi and Asami will please inform my father of this.)

"I respectfully request that none of the families left by my subordinates suffer. The only thing I am anxious about is this.

"Atmospheric pressure is increasing and I feel as if my tympanum were breaking.

"12.30 o'clock. Respiration is extraordinarily difficult. I mean I am breathing gasoline. I am intoxicated with gasoline.

"It is 12.40 o'clock."

Those were the last words written by Lieutenant Takuma Faotomu, bravest of the brave.

Very many ingenious devices have been invented to enable the crew of a stranded submarine to escape. The best-known and most widely used is some form of the air-lock or diver's chamber, as described in the chapter on the Lake boats. Through this the crew can pass in succession to the water outside and swim to the surface. If the depth is so great that an unprotected swimmer would be crushed by the weight of water above him, there is a great variety of safety-helmets, and of jackets with mouth-pieces leading to tanks containing enough air under moderate pressure to inflate the lungs and cheeks so

Accidents and Safety Devices 131

that the internal pressure of the body will counteract that of the water. An escaping seaman, burdened with such a device, cannot rise unaided to the surface but must climb or be hauled up by a rope let down from above. Moreover, he must not ascend too rapidly, or the pressure within his body will dangerously exceed that without, as if he had been suddenly picked up at the seashore and carried to the top of the Andes. The human body is too delicate and elaborate a structure to be carelessly turned into a compressed-air tank. The surplus oxygen forms bubbles which try to force their way out through the tissues of the body, causing intense pain, and possibly paralysis or death. To avoid this, divers are brought up from any great depth by slow and careful stages, unless they can be placed at once in specially-constructed tanks on shore, where the pressure they are under can be gradually reduced to normal.

Courtesy of the Scientific American.

One Type of Safety-jacket.

A covered lifeboat carried in a socket on the submarine's deck, so that in case of accidental stranding the crew could get into the small boat from below, close the hatch cover, release the lifeboat from within, and rise safely and comfortably to the surface, was an attractive feature of the *Plongeur* in 1863, and of many projected but unbuilt submarines since then. A detachable conning-tower, containing a small lifeboat that could be launched after the safety compartment had risen to the surface, has also been designed and patented more than once. Theoretically, these devices seem admirable but naval architects will have none of them. The reason for this is very simple. A submarine is primarily a warship, an instrument of destruction, and its carrying capacity is too limited to permit several hundredweight of torpedoes or supplies being crowded out by a lifeboat or a score of safety-helmets. A divers' compartment and one or two ordinary diving-suits — for these things are of military value — and a buoy that can be sent up to mark the spot where the boat has gone down are as much as you can expect to find in the average naval submarine.

One of the most instructive accidents that ever happened to an undersea boat was the loss and rescue of the German *U-3*. She sank to the bottom of Kiel Harbor on January 17, 1911. A small spherical buoy was released and rose to the surface, where it was picked up and a telephone attached to the end of the thin wire cable.

"Hello!"

"Hello! This is the captain of the *U-3* speaking. We cannot rise, but we are resting easy and have air enough to last forty-eight hours."

"Good. The steam salvage-dock *Vulcan* has been sent for and will be here before then, Herr Kapitan."

But before the *Vulcan* arrived, it occurred to some one in authority to attempt to raise the *U-3* with a large float-

Accidents and Safety Devices 133

ing crane then available. The strong steel chain ready coiled at the lower end of the buoy-line was drawn up and made fast to the crane, which could not lift the 300-ton submarine bodily, but succeeded in hauling up its bow sufficiently for the twenty-seven petty officers and seamen on board the *U-3* to be shot up through the torpedo tube to the surface. The captain and his two lieutenants chose to remain. Shortly afterwards the chain slipped and broke off one of the boat's ventilators, letting water into the hull and drowning all three officers.

Then the sea-going, steam salvage-dock *Vulcan* reached the scene and brought the *U-3* to the surface in three hours.

"The *Vulcan* is a double-hulled vessel, 230 feet in length with a lifting capacity of 500 tons. The width between the two hulls is sufficient to admit with good clearance the largest submarines. At a suitable height a shelf is formed along each wall of the interior opening, and upon this rests the removable floor of the dock. The two hulls of the ship are each built with water-tight compartments of large capacity, similar to those which are found in the side walls of the ordinary floating dock. When a sunken submarine is to be raised, the *Vulcan* steams to the wreck and is moored securely in position above it. Spanning the well between the two hulls are two massive gantry cranes, each provided with heavy lifting tackle driven by electric motors. The first operation is to fill the compartments until the vessel has sunk to the required depth. The floor of the dock is then moved clear of the well. The lifting tackles are now lowered and made fast, either to chains which have been slung around the body of the submarine, or to two massive eyebolts which are permanently riveted into the submarine's hull. At the order to hoist away, the submarine is lifted free from the mud and drawn up within the well, until its bottom is clear of the supporting shelves on the inner faces of the two hulls, above referred to.

Courtesy of the Scientific American.
The *Vulcan* salvaging the *U-3*.

The dock floor is then placed in position on the shelves, the water is pumped out of the two hulls, and the *Vulcan* rises, lifting the submarine and the dock floor clear of the water." [1]

A similar vessel was built by the French government as a result of public indignation over the delay in raising the sunken *Pluviôse*.
Great Britain has a salvage dock with a lifting capacity of 1000 tons. But the most remarkable craft of this kind belongs to Italy and was designed by the famous engineer Major Cesare Laurenti, technical director of the Fiat-San Giorgio works, builders of some of the world's best submarines. She is a twin-hulled vessel, fitted not only to pick a sunken submarine from the sea bottom, but

[1] "Scientific American," January 28, 1911, page 87.

Accidents and Safety Devices   135

to care for it in every way, for she is also a floating drydock, capable of repairing two of the largest submarines, besides being a fully equipped mother-ship for a flotilla of six. With the ends of her central tunnel closed by a false stem and stern, and propelled by twin screws driven by powerful Diesel engines, she is a fast and seaworthy vessel, capable of keeping company with her flotilla on a surface cruise. She carries a sufficient armament of quick-firing guns to beat off a hostile destroyer. But the most noteworthy feature of the Laurenti dock is a long steel cylinder, capable of enduring great pressure from within, that is used to test the resisting strength of new submarines. A new boat, or a section of a proposed new type, is placed in this tube, which is filled with water that is then compressed by pumps, reproducing the effect of submergence to any desired depth.

The United States navy tests each new submarine built for it by actually lowering the boat, with no one in it, to a depth of 200 feet. We have no Laurenti dock, no *Vulcan,* no sea-going salvage dock of any kind. The tender *Fulton* has a powerful crane, but she cannot be on the Atlantic and Pacific coasts and in the Far East, simultaneously.

" The difficulties encountered in raising the sunken British submarine *A-3,*" wrote Mr. R. G. Skerrett in the " Scientific American " some years ago, " have in them a note of warning for us. We are steadily adding to our flotilla of under-water boats, and yet we have no proper facilities in the government service for the prompt salvage of any of these boats should they be carried suddenly to the bottom. We have been fortunate so far in escaping serious accidents, but that is no reason for assuming that we are any more likely to be immune from disaster than any other naval service. We should profit by the catastrophes which have befallen England, Russia, France, Germany, and Japan, and no longer continue unprepared for kindred mishaps." [2]

We refused to profit and we continued unprepared. Then came a brief official cablegram from Hawaii, "Honolulu, March 25, 1915. U. S. submarine *F-4* left tender at 9 A.M. for submerged run. Failed to return to surface."

The other two submarines on the station and motor-boats from the tender *Alert* cruised about till they found the spot where oil and air-bubbles were coming to the surface. Two tugs then swept the bottom with a two-thousand foot sweep of chains and wire cables, which caught early the next morning on what proved to be the lost submarine, in three hundred feet of water, about a mile and a half outside the entrance to Honolulu Harbor.

For twenty-four hours or so the navy department held out the hope that the men on board her were still alive and might be rescued. But there was nothing ready to rescue them with. Three weeks were spent in building the windlasses for an improvised salvage-dock made out of two mud scows. In the meanwhile, a detachment of the department's most skilled divers were sent out from the Brooklyn Navy Yard. With their aid, strong wire cables were passed under the submarine's

[2] "Scientific American," November 23, 1912.

Accidents and Safety Devices 137

hull. While engaged on this work, one of the divers, Chief Gunner's Mate Frank Crilley, broke all deep submergence records by descending to a depth of 288 feet. As a result, his lungs were severely injured and he soon afterwards developed pneumonia.

The wire ropes chafed through and were replaced by chains. Then the *F-4* was lifted from the bottom and towed inshore to a depth of fifty feet. Here a heavy storm set in and the lines had to be cast off. Six big cylindrical-shaped pontoons were then built at San Francisco and brought out to Honolulu on the cruiser *Maryland*. Divers passed fresh chains under the *F-4*, the pontoons were sunk on either side of her, and coupled together. Then the water was blown out of the pontoons by compressed-air piped down from above, the *F-4* was raised to the surface, and towed into dry dock.

No decipherable written record was discovered inside her hull, which was filled with sand washed in through a large hole made in the plating by the chafing of the chains. But the story of the disaster was written in the plates and rivets of the vessel herself, and skilfully deduced and reconstructed by a board of inquiry, headed by Rear-Admiral Boush. Their report, which was not made public till October 27, told dramatically how the corroded condition of the lead lining in the battery tanks had let the acid eat away the rivets in the port wall of the forward tank. Salt water thus entered part of the battery, producing chlorin gas, which exploded violently, admitting more water, till the submarine began to sink by the head, in spite of the raising of her diving-rudders.

"Automatic blow was tripped, and blow valve on

auxiliary tank opened in the endeavor to check downward momentum. Manœuvering with propellers probably took place. The appreciable length of time requisite for air to build up in ballast tanks for the expulsion of sufficient quantities of water resulted in the vessel reaching crushing depth.

"Seams of the vessel began to open, and probably through open torpedo tubes and seams water entered the vessel and a condition of positive buoyancy was never attained.

"There followed actual disaster. The vessel began filling with water. The personnel abandoned stations and many sought refuge in the engine room, closing the door. Under great pressure the engine room bulkhead failed suddenly, leaving the vessel on the bottom, completely flooded."

All the boats of the "F" class had already been withdrawn from the service, by order of Secretary Daniels. Their place at Honolulu was taken by four boats of the "K" class, which made the 2100 mile voyage out from San Francisco under their own power.

CHAPTER XI

MINES

THE MINE SWEEPERS

       " 'Ware mine!"
"Starboard your helm." . . . "Full speed ahead!"
The squat craft duly swings —
A hand's breadth off, a thing of dread
The sullen breaker flings.

Carefully, slowly, patiently,
The men of Grimsby Town
Grope their way on the rolling sea —
The storm-swept, treacherous, gray North Sea —
Keeping the death-rate down.
   — H. INGAMELLS, in the "London Spectator."

A MINE is a torpedo that has no motive-power of its own but is either anchored or set adrift in the supposed path of an enemy's ship. We have already seen how Bushnell used drifting mines at Philadelphia in 1777. Anchored mines are among the many inventions of Robert Fulton. The following description of the original type, illustrated by an engraving made by himself, is taken from Fulton's " Torpedo War and Submarine Explosions."

"Plate II represents the anchored torpedo, so arranged as to blow up a vessel which should run against it; *B* is a copper case two feet long, twelve inches diameter, capable of containing one hundred pounds of powder. *A* is a brass box, in which there is a lock similar to a common gun lock, with a barrel two inches long, to contain a musket charge of powder: the box,

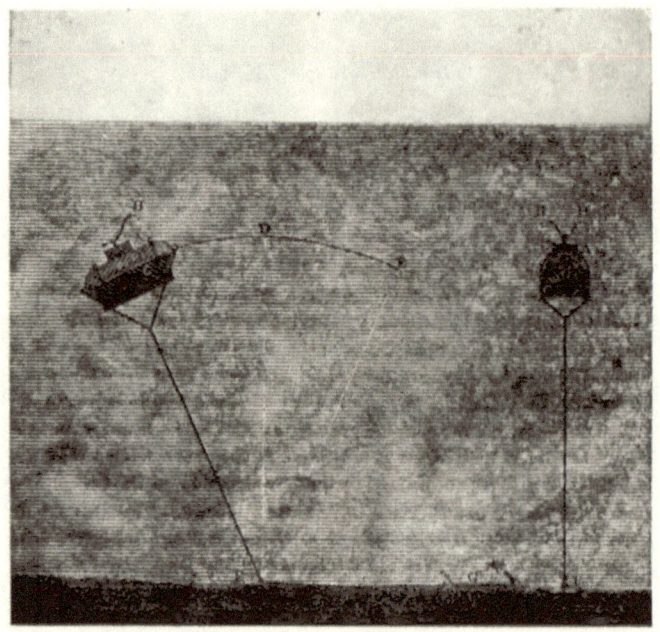

Fulton's Anchored Torpedoes.

with the lock cocked and barrel charged, is screwed to the copper case *B*. *H* is a lever which has a communication to the lock inside of the box, and in its present state holds the lock cocked and ready to fire. *C* is a deal box filled with cork, and tied to the case *B*. The object of the cork is to render the torpedo about fifteen

Mines

or twenty pounds specifically lighter than water, and give it a tendency to rise to the surface. It is held down to any given depth under water by a weight of fifty or sixty pounds as at F: there is also a small anchor G, to prevent a strong tide moving it from its position. With torpedoes prepared, and knowing the depth of water in all our bays and harbors, it is only necessary to fix the weight F at such a distance from the torpedo, as when thrown into the water, F will hold it ten, twelve, or fifteen feet below the surface at low water, it will then be more or less below the surface at high water, or at different times of the tide; but it should never be so deep as the usual draft of a frigate or ship-of-the-line. When anchored, it will, during the flood tide, stand in its present position; at slack water it will stand perpendicular to the weight F, as at D; during the ebb it will be at E. At ten feet under water the waves, in boisterous weather, would have little or no tendency to disturb the torpedo; for that if the hollow of a wave should sink ten feet below what would be the calm surface, the wave would run twenty feet high, which I believe is never the case in any of our bays and harbors. All the experience which I have on this kind of torpedo is, that in the month of October, 1805, I had one of them anchored nine feet under water, in the British Channel near Dover; the weather was severe, the waves ran high, it kept its position for twenty-four hours, and, when taken up, the powder was dry and the lock in good order. The torpedo thus anchored, it is obvious, that if a ship in sailing should strike the lever H, the explosion would be instantaneous, and she be immediately destroyed; hence, to defend our bays or harbors, let a hundred, or more if necessary, of these engines be anchored in the channel, as for example, the Narrows, to defend New York.

"The figure to the right of the plate is an end view of the torpedo. *H-H* shews its lever forked, to give the better chance of being struck.

"Having described this instrument in a way which I hope will be understood," continues Fulton, "I may be permitted to put the following question to my reader, which is: Knowing that the explosion of one hundred pounds of powder, or more if required, under the bottom of a ship-of-the-line, would destroy her, and seeing, that if a ship in sailing should strike the lever of an anchored torpedo, she would be blown up, would he have the courage, or shall I say the temerity, to sail into a channel where one or more hundred of such engines were anchored? I rely on each gentleman's sense of prudence and self-preservation, to answer this question to my satisfaction. Should the apprehension of danger become as strong on the minds of those who investigate this subject as it is on mine, we may reasonably conclude that the same regard to self-preservation will make an enemy cautious in approaching waters where such engines are placed; for however brave sailors may be, there is no danger so distressing to the mind of a seaman, or so calculated to destroy his confidence, as that which is invisible and instantaneous destruction."

But Admiral Farragut at Mobile Bay, half a century later, did have the "temerity to sail into a channel where one or more hundred of such engines were anchored." The monitor *Tecumseh* struck and exploded a mine that sent her to the bottom with almost her entire crew. The rest of the fleet began to waver when, from the main-rigging of the *Hartford* Farragut shouted his immortal command:

"Full steam ahead! Damn the torpedoes!"

As the flagship led the way through the mine field, those on board heard mine after mine bump against her bottom, but though the levers were struck and the primers

Sinking of the U. S. S. *Tecumseh*, by a Confederate mine, in Mobile Bay.

snapped, the powder-charges failed to explode. Hastily improvised out of beer-kegs and other receptacles, with tin or iron covers that became rusty and useless soon after they were placed under water, many of the Confederate mines were in this respect inferior to the well-built copper torpedoes of Fulton. Yet crude as they were, they destroyed more than forty Northern warships, transports, and supply vessels.

Percussion-caps instead of flintlocks were now used to explode contact mines. A new type of anchored torpedo, set off by an electric spark through a wire running to an operator on shore, was also a favorite with the Confederates. Because they are exploded not by contact with the ship's hull but by the closing of the circuit by the operator when he observes an enemy's vessel to be above one of them, these are called "observation mines." In the Civil War, many effective mines of this sort were

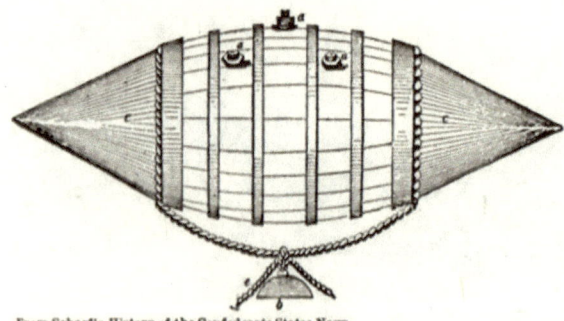

From Scharf's History of the Confederate States Navy.
A Confederate "Keg-Torpedo."

made out of whisky demijohns. One of these blew up the gunboat *Cairo,* in the Yazoo River, in the autumn of 1862. The double-ended, river gunboat *Commodore Jones* was blown to pieces by an observation mine, whose operator was subsequently captured and tied to the cutwater of another Federal gunboat as a warning and a hostage. During the bombardment of Fort Sumter by the United States fleet in 1863, the *New Ironsides* lay for an hour directly above an observation mine made of boiler iron and containing a ton of gunpowder but which failed to explode despite all the efforts of the operator. He was naturally accused of treachery and it would have gone hard with him had it not been discovered, soon after the *New Ironsides* ceased firing and stood out to sea, that the shore end of the wire had been severed by the wheel of an ammunition wagon.

During the Franco-Prussian War, the powerful French fleet blockaded the German coast but did not attack the shore batteries, which were well protected by mines.

U. S. IRON-CLAD "CAIRO" (BLOWN UP BY CONFEDERATE TORPEDO).
From Scharf's History of the Confederate States Navy.

First Warship Destroyed by a Mine.

After peace was declared the foreign consuls at one of the North German seaports congratulated the burgomaster on having planted and taken up so many mines without a single accident. Unknown to any one, the prudent burgomaster had unloaded them first, and they kept the French away just as well.

In the Spanish-American War, Admiral Dewey was able to enter Manila Bay and destroy the Spanish squadron there because its commander " had repeatedly asked

146 The Story of the Submarine

for torpedoes (mines) from Madrid, but had received none and his attempts to make them had been failures."[1]

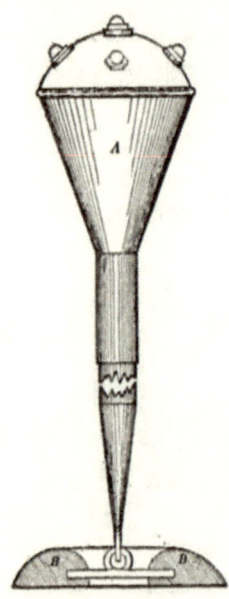

From Scharf's History of the Confederate States Navy.

A Confederate "Buoyant Torpedo" or Contact-mine.

It was the mine fields and not the feeble shore batteries that kept Sampson's fleet out of Havana and Santiago. At Guantanamo, now a United States naval station, the *Texas* and the *Marblehead* each "struck her propeller against a contact mine, which failed to explode only because it was incrusted with a thick growth of barnacles. Gratitude for the vessels' escape may fairly be divided between divine care to which the gallant and devout Captain Philip attributed it in his report, and the Spaniards' neglect to maintain a proper inspection of these defenses. A number of these torpedoes, which were of French manufacture, and contained forty-six and a half kilograms (one hundred and two pounds) of guncotton, were afterward dragged up in the channel."[2]

At the siege of Port Arthur in 1904, the Japanese fleet planted mines outside the harbor to keep the Russians in, and the Russians came out and planted mines of their own to entrap the blockaders. While engaged in this work, the Russian mine-layer *Yenisei* had a mine which

[1] Titherington's History of the Spanish-American War, p. 139.
[2] *Ibid.*, page 202.

had just been lowered through her specially constructed sternports thrown by a wave against her rudder, and was blown to atoms by the consequent explosion of three hundred more in her hold. The flagship *Petropavlosk*, returning from a sortie on April 13, struck a Japanese contact-mine and went down with the loss of six hundred men, including Vereshchagin, the famous painter of war-scenes, and Admiral Makàroff, who was not only the commander but the heart and soul of the Russian fleet.[3] A month later, another mine cost the Japanese their finest battleship, the *Hatsuse*. Nor was the loss confined either to the belligerents or to the duration of the war. Nearly one hundred Chinese and other neutral merchant vessels were sunk by some of the many mines torn loose from their anchors by storms to drift, the least noticeable and most terrible of derelicts, over all the seas of the Far East, long after peace was declared.

The same thing on a larger scale will doubtless take place as a result of the present European War. From the Baltic to the Dardanelles, both sides have sown the waters thick with contact mines, hundreds of which have already broken loose and been cast up on the shores of Denmark, Holland, and other neutral lands. How many more have been picked up on the coasts of the different belligerent countries, the military censors have naturally kept a close secret; how many of these infernal machines are now drifting about the North Sea, the North Atlantic, and the Mediterranean it is impossible to compute. Scarcely a week passes without the publication of such

[3] He had done notable work with mines himself, during the Russo-Turkish War of 1878.

news items as the following extracts from "Current events in Norway," in the "American-Scandinavian Review" for July-August, 1915:

"One hundred and fifty mines had been brought into Bergen up to April 12. The steamer *Caprivi* of Bergen, which sank after being struck by a mine off the coast of Ireland, was on its way from Baltimore with a cargo of 4150 tons of grain, the property of the Norwegian government. . . . The German government has declared its willingness to comply with the demand of the Norwegian government for compensation for the *Belridge,* provided it be proved that the sinking of the steamer was the result of a German torpedo. The pieces of the shell found in the side of the vessel are to be sent to the German government, and in case there should be any disagreement about the facts they will be submitted to arbitration."

Unfortunately in most cases where a neutral ship is so sunk, the exploding mine automatically destroys all evidence of its own origin, and each belligerent promptly and positively declares that it must have been planted, if not deliberately set adrift, by the other side. The neutral is left to get what satisfaction he can out of the ruling of the last Hague Conference that all contact mines must be so constructed as to become harmless after breaking loose from their moorings. There is nothing mechanically difficult about installing such a safety device, and all the great powers now at war with each other solemnly pledged themselves to do so. But the temptation of perhaps destroying a hostile battleship as the

Hatsuse was destroyed, by a drifting mine, has apparently been too great.

Premature explosion of the mine during handling and planting, such as caused the destruction of the *Yenisei* is, of course, carefully guarded against. One of the simplest and most effective safety devices is that used in the British navy, where the external parts of the exploding apparatus are sealed with a thick layer of sugar, which is dissolved by the sea-water after being submerged for a few minutes. By then the mine-laying vessel has had time to get safely out of the neighborhood.

Modern mines are of various shapes and sizes but are as a rule either spherical or shaped like a pear with the stem down. The anchor is a hollow, flat-bottomed cylinder, containing its own anchor cable wound on a windlass, and making a convenient base or stand for the explosive chamber or mine proper, so that the whole apparatus can be stood or trundled about the deck of a mine-layer like a barrel. Once placed in the water either by being dropped through the overhanging stern-ports of a large sea-going mine-planter like the U.S.S. *San Francisco,* or lowered over the side of a smaller craft by a derrick boom, the weight of its anchor causes the mine to assume an upright position. This releases a small weight or plummet at the end of a short line attached to a spring that keeps the windlass inside the anchor from revolving. When the plummet has sunk to the end of its cord, its weight pulls down the spring, and the windlass begins to revolve and unreel the cable,

150   The Story of the Submarine

the end of which is, of course, made fast to the bottom of the mine. This causes the anchor, which has been held up by the buoyancy of the mine, to sink, and follows the plummet till the latter touches the bottom. Freed of the plummet's weight, the spring now flies up and stops the windlass. But the hollow anchor is now

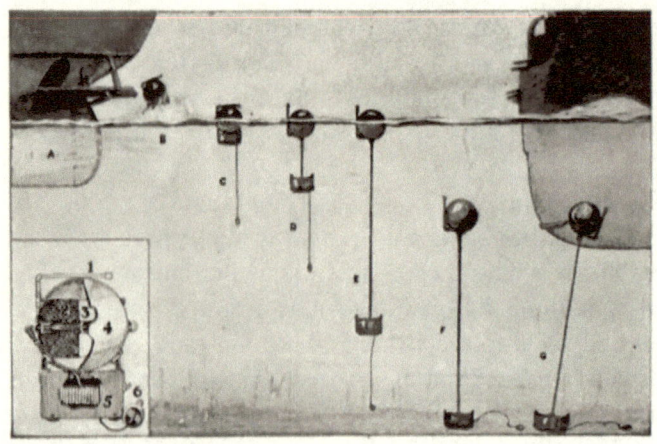

(Redrawn from the London Sphere.)

Modern Contact-Mine.

A, Mine-Planter; B, Mine being dropped overboard; C, Plummet-line extended; D, Anchor sinking; E, Plummet touching bottom; F, Mine submerged and anchored; G, Battleship striking mine; 1, The "Striker"; 2, Charge of Explosives; 3, Air-space, for Buoyancy; 4, Mine-case; 5, Anchor; 6, Plummet.

filled with water, whose additional weight drags the mine under. When the anchor rests on the bottom, the mine will be at the same distance beneath the surface of the water as the anchor had to sink after the windlass stopped, or the length of the plummet's line. By regulating that, a mine can be made automatically to set itself at any desired depth.

Mines

Mines are almost never laid singly but in groups, the area of water so planted being called a "mine field." A secret, zigzag channel is often left clear for the benefit of friendly craft. The rows of mines are usually "staggered" or placed like the men on a checker-board, so that if a hostile vessel passes through an opening in the first row she will strike a mine in the second. Another device is to couple together the mooring cables of two or more mines so that a ship passing between them will draw them in against her sides.

Contact may cause explosion in any one of several different ways. The head or sides of the mine may be studded with projecting rods like the striker on the nose of a Whitehead, to be either driven directly in against a detonating charge of fulminate or else open the jaws of a clutch and release the spring of a firing-pin. Such external movable parts, however, are too prone to become overgrown and clogged with barnacles and the like. A more modern way is to have the shock of the collision with the ship's hull dislodge a heavy ball held in a cup inside the mine. The fall of this weight sets in motion machinery which fires the detonating charge. Or the device may not be mechanical but electrical, as in the type of mine that, when drawn far enough over to one side by a vessel passing over it, spills a cupful of mercury. This stream of liquid metal closes an electric circuit, so that an electric current passes through a piece of platinum wire embedded in fulminate and heats it red-hot, with obvious results. This current may be obtained either from a storage-battery carried in the mine itself, or through a wire running down the mooring cable and over the bottom to the shore. Most shore-control mines are so designed that they can either be fired by observation, or else turned into electro-contact mines of the above-mentioned type by arranging the switches in the controlling station. It is also possible to have the contact serve to warn the operator on shore by ringing a bell and indicating the position of the intruding ship in the mine-field.

Just as barbed-wire entanglements on land are blown out of the way by small charges of high explosives, so mined areas of the sea can be cleared by "counter-mining." One or more strings of linked-together mines, of a small, easily-handled type, are carefully placed by light-draft vessels in the waters already planted by the enemy. When these are exploded together, the concussion is enough to destroy any anchored mines near at hand, either by setting off their exploding-devices or causing their cases to leak, so that they will be filled with water and sink harmlessly to the bottom. Or a channel may be cleared by "sweeping" it with a drag-rope towed along the bottom by two small steamers, exploding the mines or tearing them up by the roots. Very effective work of this kind has been done by the small steam-trawlers used by the North Sea fishermen, and if anything of the sort is ever necessary in American waters we may be thankful for the powerful sea-going tugs now towing strings of barges up and down our coasts.

But even a light field-piece on shore can shell and sink the sort of small, unarmored craft that must be used for mine-sweeping. When a fleet attacks a channel or harbor entrance properly defended by both mine-fields

U. S. Mine-planter *San Francisco.*

and batteries, each supporting the other, there comes a time when the naval forces must wait till troops can be landed to drive away the forces protecting the rear of the batteries, so that the mine-sweepers can advance and clear a channel for the superdreadnoughts. The most striking example of this is the holding of the Allied fleet by the Turks at the Dardanelles.

There, too, effective use is being made of the latest, which is an adaptation of the oldest type of torpedo: the drifting mine.[4] This twentieth-century improvement on Bushnell's "kegs charged with powder" floats upright, with a vertical-acting propeller on top and another on its bottom, and a hydrostatic valve set to maintain it at any desired depth. Should it rise or sink, the change in pressure will cause the valve to act on the principle already explained in connection with the Whitehead torpedo (see page 44). Controlled by the valve, the little compressed-air motor attached to the vertical propellers will cause them to make a few revolutions, just enough to keep the mine at a constant depth beneath the surface of the Dardanelles, as the four-mile-an-hour current carries it down against the Anglo-French fleet. Within a few hours of each other, during the furious bombardment of the forts on March 18, 1915, the French battleship *Bouvet* was struck by one of these drifting mines and went down stern-foremost, then H.M.S. *Ocean* was sunk by another, and the *Irresistible* forced to run ashore to escape sinking, only to be pounded to pieces by the guns of the forts. A feature of this type of mine is that its

[4] This was a very popular type with the Confederate Torpedo Service in the Civil War.

Mines

size and shape enable it to be launched through a torpedo tube, either from a surface craft or from a submarine.

Ordinary contact-mines, without anchors and attached to floats that hold them a few feet below the surface of the water, are sometimes dropped overboard from a vessel closely pursued by an enemy. A small mine so dropped by a German light cruiser returning from an attempted raid on the English coast, early in the war, was struck by the pursuing British submarine *D*-5 and sent her to the bottom. The *D*-5 was running awash at the time and only two officers and two seamen were saved.

CHAPTER XII

THE SUBMARINE IN ACTION

"Hit and hard hit! The blow went home
The muffled knocking stroke,
The steam that overrides the foam,
The foam that thins to smoke,
The smoke that cloaks the deep aboil,
The deep that chokes her throes,
Till, streaked with ash and sleeked with oil,
The lukewarm whirlpools close!"
— KIPLING.

THE first submarine in history to sink a hostile warship without also sinking herself is the *E-9* of the British navy. Together with most of her consorts, she was sent, at the outbreak of the present war, to explore and reconnoiter off the German coast and the island fortress of Heligoland to find where the enemy's ships were lying, how they were protected and how they might be attacked. After six weeks of such work, the *E-9* entered Heligoland Bight on September 13, 1914, and discharged two torpedoes at the German light cruiser *Hela*. One exploded against her bow and the other amidships, and the cruiser went down almost immediately, drowning many of her crew.

Another British submarine had already appeared in action off Heligoland but as a saver instead of a destroyer of human life. On the 28th of August a number

English Submarine Rescuing English Sailors.

of German torpedo-craft and light cruisers were decoyed out to sea by the appearance and pretended flight of some English destroyers. (It has been declared but not officially confirmed that the "bait" consisted not of destroyers but two British submarines, which rose to the surface where one of them pretended to be disabled and was slowly towed away by the other till their pursuers were almost within range, when the line was cast off and both boats dived to safety.) The Germans found themselves attacked by a larger British flotilla and a confused sort of battle followed. During the mêlée, an English cruiser lowered a whaleboat that picked up several survivors of a sunken German vessel. The cruiser was then driven away by a more powerful German ship, and the crew of the whaleboat found themselves left in the enemy's waters without arms, food, or navigating instruments, Suddenly a periscope rose out of the water alongside, followed by the conning-tower and hull of the British submarine *E-4*, which took the Englishmen on board and left the Germans the whaleboat, after which both parties went home rejoicing.

Shortly after this, the German submarine *U-15* boldly attacked a British squadron, but revealed herself by the white wake of her periscope as it cut through the calm water. A beautifully aimed shot from the cruiser *Birmingham* smashed the periscope. The submarine dived, temporarily safe but blinded, for she was an old-fashioned craft with only one observation instrument. Her commander now essayed a swift "porpoise dive" up to the surface and down again, exposing only the conning-tower for a very few seconds. But a broadside blazed

Engagement between the *Birmingham* and the *U-15*.
1. Submarine's periscope shot away.
2. Submarine dives, temporarily safe but blinded.
3. Submarine exposes conning-tower.
4. Conning-tower shot away, *U-15* sinking.

from the *Birmingham,* a shell struck squarely against the conning-tower, and the sea poured in through the ragged death-wound in the deck of the *U-15.*

But these early affairs were now overshadowed as completely as the first Union victories in West Virginia were overshadowed by Bull Run. Another British squadron encountered another German submarine and this time the periscope was not detected. Lieutenant-Commander Otto von Weddigen had had ample time to take up an ideal position beside the path of his enemies, who passed in slow and stately procession before the bow torpedo-tubes of the *U-9.* The German officer pressed a button and saw through his periscope the white path of the "Schwartzkopf" as it sped straight and true to the tall side of the *Aboukir.* He saw the cruiser heaved into the air by the shock of the bursting war-head, then watched her settle and go down. Round swung her nearest consort to the rescue, lowering her lifeboats as she came. But scarcely had the survivors of the *Aboukir's* company set foot on the deck of the *Hogue* than she, too, was torpedoed, and the half-naked men of both crews went tumbling down the slope of the upturned side as she rolled over and sank. Up steamed the *Cressy,* her gun-crews standing by their useless pieces, splendid in helpless bravery. Half reluctantly, von Weddigen sent his remaining foe to the bottom and slipped away under the waves, the victor of the strangest naval battle in history.

Not a German had received the slightest injury; fourteen hundred Englishmen had been killed. It was the loss of these trained officers and seamen, and not that of three old cruisers that would soon have been sent to the scrap heap, that was felt by the British navy. Realizing that no fears for their own lives would keep the officers of a British ship from attempting to rescue the drowning crew of another, the Admiralty issued the following order:

"It has been necessary to point out for the future guidance of his Majesty's ships that the conditions that prevail when one vessel of a squadron is injured in a mine-field or exposed to submarine attack are analogous to those which occur in an action and that the rule of leaving disabled ships to their own resources is applicable, so far at any rate as large vessels are concerned. No act of humanity, whether to friend or foe, should lead to a neglect of the proper precautions and dispositions of war, and no measures can be taken to save life which prejudice the military situation."

Another old cruiser, the *Hermes,* that had been turned into a floating base for sea-planes, was torpedoed off Dunkirk by a German submarine, most of the crew being rescued by French torpedo boats. On New Year's day, 1915, the battleship *Formidable* was likewise sent to the bottom of the English Channel. She too was a rather old ship, of the same class as the *Bulwark,* which had been destroyed by an internal explosion two weeks earlier in the Medway, and the *Irresistible,* afterwards sunk by a mine in the Dardanelles.

But there was nothing small or old about the *Audacious.* She was — or is — a 24,800 ton superdreadnought, launched in 1911 and carrying ten thirteen-and-a-half-inch guns. This stupendous war-engine was found rolling helpless in the Irish Sea, her after compartments flooded by a great hole made either by a drifting mine or, what is more likely considering its position, by a torpedo from a German submarine. The White Star liner *Olympic,* which had been summoned by wireless, took the disabled warship in tow for several hours, after which the *Audacious* was cast off and abandoned. A photograph taken by one of the *Olympic's* passengers and afterwards widely circulated shows the huge ironclad down by the stern, listing heavily to one side, and apparently on the point of sinking. But her loss has never been admitted by the British Admiralty, and it has been repeatedly declared by reputable persons that the *Audacious* was kept afloat till the *Olympic* was out of sight, and was then towed by naval vessels into Belfast, where she was drydocked and repaired at Harland and Wolff's shipyard to be sent back to the fighting line. Her fate is one of the most interesting of the many mysteries of the war and will probably not be made clear till peace has come. The silence of the British Admiralty is explained by the standing orders forbidding the revealing of the whereabouts of any of his Majesty's ships, particularly when helpless and disabled. It should be noted in this connection that the German government has never admitted the loss of the battleship *Pommern* which the Russians insist was sunk by one of their submarines in the Baltic.

Because the overwhelming strength of the Allied fleet has kept the German and Austrian battleships safely locked up behind shore batteries, mine-fields and nettings, the Allies' submarines have had comparatively few targets to try their skill on. The activity of the British submarines in the North Sea at the outbreak of the war

Sinking of the *Aboukir, Cressy,* and *Hogue.*

Copyright, Illustrated London News & N. Y. Sun.

has already been referred to, and a year later they found another opportunity in the Baltic. There the German fleet had the same preponderance over the Russian as the English had over the German battleships in the North Sea, but the British dreadnoughts could not be sent through the long tortuous passage of the Skagerrack and Cattegat, thick-sown with German mines, without cutting the British fleet in half and giving the Germans a splendid chance to defeat either half and then slip back through the Kiel Canal and destroy the other. So England sent some of her submarines instead. One of these joined the Russian squadron defending the Gulf of Riga against a German fleet and decided the fight by disabling the great battle-cruiser *Moltke*. Another, the *E-13*, ran ashore on the Danish island of Saltholm on August 19, 1915, and was warned by the commander of a Danish torpedo-boat that she would be allowed twenty-four hours to get off. Before the time-limit had expired and while three Danish torpedo-boats were standing by, two German destroyers steamed up, torpedoed the *E-13*, and killed half her crew by gun-fire: an outrageous violation of Denmark's neutrality.[1]

[1] London, Jan. 4.— A British official statement issued to-day says:

"Sir Edward Grey, secretary for foreign affairs, has answered the complaint by the Germans through the American embassies regarding the destruction off the coast of Ireland of a German submarine and crew, by the British auxiliary *Baralong*, by referring to various German outrages.

"Sir Edward Grey offers to submit such incidents, including the *Baralong* case, to an impartial tribunal composed, say, of officers of the United States navy.

"The Foreign Office has presented to the House of Commons the full correspondence between Ambassador Page and Sir Edward Grey concerning the case. A memorandum from Germany concerning the sinking of the submarine includes affidavits from six Americans who

The Submarine in Action

Daredevil deeds have been done by the submarines of both sides in the Dardanelles. The little *B-11* swam up the straits, threading her way through mine-field after mine-field, her captain keeping his course by "dead-reckoning" with map and compass and stop watch. To have exposed his periscope would have drawn the fire of the many shore batteries, to have dived a few feet too far in those shallow waters would have meant running aground, to have misjudged the swirling, changing currents might have meant annihilation. But Commander Holbrook brought his vessel safely through, torpedoed and sank the guard-ship *Messudieh,* a Turkish ironclad of the vintage of 1874, and returned to receive the Victoria Cross from his king and a gigantic "Iron Cross" from his brother officers. The *E-11* went up even to Constantinople, torpedoed a Turkish transport within sight of the city and threw the whole waterfront into a panic. More transports and store-ships were sunk or driven on shore in the Sea of Marmora, a gunboat was torpedoed, and then the *Kheyr-el-din,* an old 10,000 ton battleship that had been the *Kurfürst Freiderich Wilhelm* before the kaiser sold her to Turkey, was sent to the bottom of the same waters by British submarines. One of them the *E-15* ran aground in the Dardanelles and was forced to surrender to the Turks, but before they could float her off and make use of her, two steam launches dashed upstream through the fire of the shore

were muleteers aboard the steamer *Nicosian* and witnessed the *Baralong's* destruction of the submarine. A further affidavit from Larimore Holland, of Chattanooga, Tennessee, who was a member of the crew of the *Baralong,* was submitted. All the affidavits speak of the *Baralong* as disguised and flying the American flag."

batteries and torpedoed the stranded submarine as Cushing blew up the *Albemarle*.

But on the same day as the *E-11's* first exploit — May 25, 1915, the British battleship *Triumph* went down with most of her crew off Gallipoli, torpedoed by a German submarine. The *U-51* had made the 2400 mile trip from the North Sea, using as tenders a number of small tank steamers flying the Spanish flag. These vessels intentionally drew the attention of the cordon of British destroyers drawn across the Straits of Gibraltar and were captured, while the submarine swam safely through and traversed the Mediterranean to the Dardanelles. Two days after her first exploit, the *U-51* or perhaps one of her Austrian consorts, sank another British battleship, the *Majestic,* off Gallipoli. The *U-51* has been reported sunk by Russian warships in the Black Sea.

If they could sink two battleships in three days, why did n't the German undersea boats sink a dozen or so more and raise the siege of the Dardanelles? Enver Pasha, the Turkish minister of war, declared that "the presence of the submarines destroyed all hopes of Russia's ever effectively landing troops on the coast north of Constantinople." Then why did they permit the landing of British, Australian, New Zealand, and French troops on the Gallipoli Peninsula and the plains of ancient Troy? It was not until August, 1915, that the transport *Royal Edward* was sunk in the Mediterranean by an Austrian submarine. Perhaps before this war is over some British transport may be torpedoed in the North Sea or the English Channel, but for more than a year and a half since its outbreak, troop-ships and

Tiny target afforded by Periscopes in rough weather.

Copyright, London Sphere & N. Y. Herald.

store-ships have been crossing to France as if there were not a hostile "U-boat" in the world. Equally mysterious has been the immunity of the light-draft monitors and obsolescent gunboats off the Flemish coast, where their heavy guns did so much to check the first German drive on Calais, and have harassed the invaders' right flank ever since. Many of these are mere floating platforms for one or two modern guns, all are slow-steaming, and they are not always in water too shallow for an undersea boat to swim in, yet none have been sunk by a submarine since the loss of the *Hermes,* in the autumn of 1914. Zeebrugge, the Belgian port that has been made the headquarters for German submarines in the North Sea, has been several times bombarded by the British fleet and, according to reports from Amsterdam, half-built submarines on the shore there have been destroyed by shell-fire. Why did the completed undersea boats in the harbor fail to come out and torpedo or drive away the attacking fleet? We have been shown what modern submarines can do; what prevents them from doing much more?

Shortly after von Weddigen's great exploit, a German submarine rose to the surface so near the British destroyer *Badger* that before the undersea boat could submerge again she was rammed, cut open and sunk. One of the most picturesque and least expected features of this war has been the revival of old ways; soldiers are again wearing breastplates and metal helmets and fighting with crossbows and catapults, while against the modern submarine, seamen are effectively using the most ancient of all naval weapons: the ram. It takes two minutes for the average undersea boat to submerge, during which time a thirty-knot destroyer can come charging up from a mile away, with a good chance of scoring a hit with her forward 3- or 4-inch gun, even if she gets there too late to ram. In the case of the *U-12*, the submarine dived deep enough to get her hull and superstructure out of harm's way, only to have the top of her conning-tower crushed in by the destroyer as it passed over her. When the inrush of water forced the *U-12* to rise to the surface and surrender, her crew discovered that the main hatch could not be opened because one of the periscopes had been bent down across it. Some of them succeeded in climbing out of the torpedo-hatch and jumping overboard before the *U-12* went down for good. As she sank stern foremost, it was observed that both of her bow-tubes were empty; evidence that she had vainly launched two torpedoes at the British flotilla that were hunting her down. Though several British destroyers and torpedo-boats have been sent to the bottom by German submarines, and the English *E-9* has sunk the German destroyer *S-126*, yet the nimble surface torpedo-craft have usually proved too difficult for the undersea boats to hit with their fixed tubes that can only fire straight ahead or astern.

It has been pointed out that the *Aboukir*, *Cressy* and *Hogue*, the *Formidable*, and the *Audacious* were all moving slowly and unescorted by any destroyers when they were attacked and sunk. The same was true of the *Leon Gambetta* and the *Giuseppe Garibaldi*, when they were sent to the bottom of the Mediterranean by Austrian submarines. Under modern conditions, such isolated big ships are in much the same perilous position as would have been a lonely battery of Union artillery marching through a country swarming with Confederate cavalry. While an escort of destroyers is no sure guarantee against submarine attack, their presence certainly seems to act as a powerful deterrent.

Waters suspected of containing hostile submarines are swept, very much as they would be for mines, by pairs of destroyers or steam trawlers, dragging an arrangement of strong cables between them. Sometimes this is festooned with explosives to blow in the side of any undersea boat it may touch. Usually the vessels engaged in this work use a large net. When they feel the weight of a catch, it is said that they let go the ends and leave it to the submarine's own twin propellers to entangle themselves thoroughly. An undersea boat so entrapped is helpless to do anything but either sink or else empty her tanks and try to rise and surrender. A submarine in trouble usually sends up notification in the form of large quantities of escaping oil and gas.

Inventors have been busy devising new kinds of traps, snares, and exaggerated lobster-pots to be placed in the waters about the British Isles. How many German submarines have poked their noses into these devices probably not even the British Admiralty could tell, if it was so minded, but the traps are said to have been put down very plentifully and most of the published designs are extremely ingenious.

Individual torpedo-nets for ships have rather gone out of fashion, but the most effective way of keeping submarines out of a harbor is to close its entrance with booms and nettings. The principal naval bases on both sides are undoubtedly so protected. It has been persistently reported that the immunity of British transports crossing the channel is due to a double line of booms, nets and mines stretching from one shore to the other, and enclosing a broad, safe channel outside which the "U-boats" roam hungrily. There would seem to be no great difficulty in building such a barrier, but it would be extremely difficult to keep intact in heavy weather and for that reason most of our naval officers are skeptical of its existence.

Microphones which have been placed under water off the coasts of France, Great Britain, and Ireland have succeeded in detecting the presence of submarines at a distance of fifty-five miles. This device has been perfected by the joint labors of an American electrical engineer, Mr. William Dubilier, and Professor Tissot of the French Academy of Science. These two gentlemen, experimenting with microphones and a submarine placed at their disposal by the French government, "discovered in the course of the tests that the underwater craft were sources of sound waves of exceedingly high frequency, quite distinctive from any other subaqueous sounds. While the cause of the high-pitched sound is known to the inventors, it cannot be divulged since it would then be possible for German submarine constructors to eliminate the source of the tell-tale sound waves, and thus render void the purpose of the detector installation."[1]

These microphones, it is believed, are usually arranged

[1] "Scientific American," October 16, 1915.

in a semicircle. Each instrument records sound waves best when they come from one particular direction. The operator on shore, listening to a device that eliminates all other sounds coming in from under the sea, can tell by the way a passing submarine affects the different microphones in the semicircle how far off and in what direction it is moving, and so warns and summons the ever-watchful patrol boats.

Air craft are doubtless being much used in the hunt for submarines, for an aviator at a height of several hundred feet can distinctly see a submarine swimming beneath him in clear water with a good light reflected from the bottom. Early in the war, the pilot and observer of a "Taube" that was brought down in the North Sea were rescued by a British submarine. In the attack on Cuxhaven a combined force of submarines, sea-planes, and light cruisers was resisted by the German shore-batteries, destroyers, "U-boats" aeroplanes and Zeppelins. As the British sea-planes returned from dropping bombs on the Cuxhaven navy yard or taking observations above the Kiel Canal, some of them were shot down by the Germans but the aviators were picked up, as had been arranged beforehand, by English submarines. In the spring of 1915 there was an engagement between a Zeppelin and a British submarine in which each side claimed the victory. On August 26 of the same year the secretary of the British Admiralty announced:

"Squadron Commander Arthur Bigsworth, R.N., destroyed single-handed a German submarine this morning by bombs dropped from an aeroplane. The submarine

Copyright, Illustrated London News & Flying.

Photograph of a submarine, twenty feet below the surface, taken from the aeroplane, whose shadow is shown in the picture.

was observed to be completely wrecked, and sank off Ostend.

"It is not the practice of the Admiralty to publish statements regarding the losses of German submarines, important though they have been, in cases where the enemy has no other source of information as to the time and place at which these losses have occurred. In the case referred to above, however, the brilliant feat of Squadron Commander Bigsworth was performed in the immediate neighborhood of the coast in occupation of the enemy and the position of the sunken submarine has been located by a German destroyer."

"This is inexact," replied the German Admiralty. "The submarine was attacked but not hit and returned to port undamaged. One of our submarines on August 16 destroyed by gunfire the benzol factory with the attached benzol warehouses and coke furnaces near Harrington, England. The statement of the English press that the submarine attacked the open towns of Harrington, Parton, and Whitehaven is inexact."

Equally interesting but unfortunately lacking in details are the reports from the Adriatic of submarines fighting submarines. There have been three such duels, in one an Austrian sank an Italian submarine, in another the Italian was victorious, while after the third both were found lying on the bottom, each torn open by the other's torpedo. As it is a physical impossibility for the pilot of one submarine to see another under the water, it would seem as if at least one of the combatants in each of these fights must have been running on the surface at the time.

Both Mr. Simon Lake and the late John P. Holland were absolutely confident that submarines could not fight submarines, that surface craft would be utterly unable to injure or resist them, and that therefore the submarine boat would make naval warfare impossible and do more than anything else to bring about permanent peace.

All that can be said at present is that the actual situation is much more complex than had been expected. Submarines have sunk many surface warships but have suffered heavily themselves. The German government has admitted the loss of over a dozen "U-boats," while the unofficial estimates of their enemies' run as high as thirty-five or fifty German submarines destroyed or captured. Admiral Beatty's victorious squadron, pursuing the German battle-cruisers after the second North Sea fight, turned and retreated at the wake of a single torpedo and the glimpse of hostile periscopes. But the submarine has not yet driven the surface warship from the seas and it has signally failed against transports. Its moral effect has been very great: British submarines have terrorized the citizens of Constantinople; while the victories of their beloved "U-boats" have cheered the German people as the victories of our frigates cheered us in 1812, and have been a somewhat similar shock to the nerves of the British navy. But that sturdy organization has recovered from more than one attack of nerves. And as the war goes on, it becomes increasingly clear that it is unfair to expect unsupported submarines, any more than unsupported frigates a century ago, to do the work of an entire navy. Like the aeroplane, the submarine was first derided as useless, next hailed as a complete substitute for all other arms, then found to be an indispensable auxiliary, whose scope and value are now being determined.

CHAPTER XIII

THE SUBMARINE BLOCKADE

"It is true that submarine boats have improved, but they are as useless as ever. Nevertheless, the German navy is carefully watching their progress, though it has no reason to make experiments itself."
ADMIRAL VON TIRPITZ, in 1901.

"DANGER!
Being the Log of Captain John Sirius
by
Sir Arthur Conan Doyle."

IF you have not read the above-mentioned story by the author of Sherlock Holmes, I advise you to go to the nearest public library and ask for it. For those that cannot spare the time to do this, here are a brief outline and a few quotations.

Captain John Sirius is supposed to be chief of submarines in the navy of Norland, a small European kingdom at war with England. With only eight submarines, he establishes a blockade of Great Britain and begins sinking all ships bringing in food. He enters a French harbor, though France is at peace with his country, and sinks three British ships that have taken refuge there.

"I suppose," says the captain, "they thought they were safe in French waters but what did I care about three-mile limits and international law! The view of my government was that England was blockaded, food contraband, and vessels carrying it to be destroyed. The lawyers could argue about it afterwards. My business was to starve the enemy any way I could."

Presently he overtook an American ship and sank her by gunfire as her skipper shouted protests over the rail.

"It was all the same to me what flag she flew so long as she was engaged in carrying contraband of war to the British Isles. . . . Of course I knew there would be a big row afterwards and there was."

"The terror I had caused had cleared the Channel."

"There was talk of a British invasion (of Norland) but I knew this to be absolute nonsense, for the British had learned by this time that it would be sheer murder to send transports full of soldiers to sea in the face of submarines. When they have a Channel tunnel, they can use their fine expeditionary force upon the Continent but until then it might not exist so far as Europe is concerned."

"Heavens, what would England have done against a foe with thirty or forty submarines?"

The British navy could do nothing to stop Captain John Sirius. One of his submarines was sunk by an armed liner, but with the remaining seven he sank the *Olympic* and so many other vessels that no one dared try to bring food into Great Britain. At the end of six weeks, fifty thousand people there had died of starvation and the British government had to make peace with Norland and pay for all the damage the submarines had done to neutrals.

The Submarine Blockade

As a warning to his countrymen, Sir Arthur Conan Doyle wrote this story in May, 1914. Before it was published,[1] England was at war with Germany. On February 4, 1915, the famous "War Zone Decree" was published in Berlin.

"The waters around Great Britain, including the whole of the English Channel, are declared hereby to be included within the zone of war, and after the 18th inst, all enemy merchant vessels encountered in these waters will be destroyed, even if it may not be possible always to save their crews and passengers.

"Within this war-zone neutral vessels are exposed to danger since, in view of the misuse of the neutral flags ordered by the government of Great Britain on the 31st ult., and of the hazards of naval warfare, neutral ships cannot always be prevented from suffering from the attacks intended for enemy ships.

"The routes of navigation around the north of the Shetland Islands in the eastern part of the North Sea and in a strip thirty miles wide along the Dutch coast are not open to the danger-zone."

But those routes had been closed three months before by the British government, which declared that it had had the North Sea planted with anchored contact mines, but that all ships trading to neutral ports would, if they first called at some British port, be given safe conduct to Holland or Scandinavia, by way of the English Channel. This way would run through the proposed "war-zone."

International law says nothing about either "war-zones" or submarines. In all probability, special rules

[1] In "Collier's Weekly," August 22, and 29, 1914.

for undersea warfare will be drawn up by a conference of delegates from the leading countries of the world soon after the end of the present war. But till then, no such conference can be held, and the United States has always maintained, even when it has been to its disadvantage to do so, that no one nation can change international law to suit herself. We insist that the game be played according to the rules. A submarine has no more rights than any other warship. It may sink a merchantman if the latter tries to fight or escape. If the captured vessel is found to be carrying contraband to the enemy's country, the warship may either take her into port as a prize or, if this is impracticable, sink her. But before an unarmed and unresisting merchant vessel can be sunk, the passengers and crew must be given time and opportunity to escape.

President Wilson gave notice on February 10, 1915, that if, by act of the commander of any German warship, an American vessel or the lives of American citizens should be lost on the high seas, the United States " would be constrained to hold the Imperial government of Germany to a strict accountability for such acts of their naval authorities and to take any steps that might be necessary to safeguard American lives and property and to secure to American citizens the full enjoyments of their acknowledged rights on the high seas."

On the same day, a note to Great Britain voiced our objection to the " explicit sanction by a belligerent government for its merchant ships generally to fly the flag of a neutral power within certain portions of the high

The Submarine Blockade 181

seas which are presumed to be frequented with hostile warships."

To this Sir Edward Grey replied that "the British government have no intention of advising their merchant shipping to use foreign flags as a general practice or resort to them otherwise than for escaping capture or destruction."

Such "sailing under false colors" to fool the enemy's cruisers is an old and well-established right of merchantmen of belligerent countries. Its abuse, under present-day conditions, however, might have given the German submarine commanders a plausible excuse for sinking neutral vessels. To avoid this, neutral shipowners began to paint the name, port, and national colors on the broadside of each of their steamers, plain enough to be read from afar through a periscope.

Then the time came for the war-zone decree to be put into effect, and the world watched with great interest and no little apprehension to see what the submarine blockaders could do.

Seven British ships were sunk during the first six days. Then came a lull, followed by the announcement by the British Admiralty that between February 23 to March 3, 3805 transoceanic ships had arrived at British ports, 669 had cleared and none had been lost, while two German submarines had been sunk. During the eleven weeks between the establishing of the blockade and the sinking of the *Lusitania,* forty-two oversea vessels and twenty-eight fishing boats of British registry had been sunk by the submarines, but 16,190 liners and freighters had safely run the blockade. The largest number of vessels sunk by the "U-boats" in any one week was thirty-six, be-

German Submarine Pursuing English Merchantman.
(Note stern torpedo-tubes, and funnel for carrying off exhaust from Diesel engine.)

tween June 23 and 30; while nineteen British merchantmen, with a total tonnage of 76,000, and three fishing vessels were destroyed either by submarines or mines during the week ending August 25. The total number sunk in the first six months was 485. But with more than fifteen hundred ships coming and going every week, the submarine blockade of the British Isles was obviously a failure.

It was a costly failure from the military point of view. The expenditure of torpedoes alone must have been considerable and a modern Whitehead or Schwartzkopf costs from five to eight thousand dollars and takes several months to build. How many of the "U-boats" themselves have fallen prey to the British patroling craft, traps, mines, and drag-nets cannot be computed with any accuracy, but by the first of September, 1915, the number declared to be lost "on the authority of a high official in the British Admiralty" ran anywhere from thirty to fifty. Even if she has been completing a new submarine every week since the war began, Germany cannot afford the loss of so much material, and still, less, of so many trained men. Captain Persius, one of the foremost German writers on naval affairs, pointed this out in a newspaper article that brought a hurricane of angry criticism about his ears. How great has been the wear and tear on the nervous systems of the submarine crews is shown by the following extract from the statement of Captain Hansen of the captured *U-16*.

"It is fearfully trying on the nerves. Not every man can endure it. While running under the sea there is deathlike stillness in the boats, as the electrical machinery is noiseless. . . . As the air becomes heated it gets poor and mixed with the odor of oil from the machinery.

The atmosphere becomes fearful. An overpowering sleepiness often attacks new men and one requires the utmost will power to keep awake. I have had men who did not want to eat during the first three days out because they did not want to lose that amount of time from sleep. Day after day spent in such cramped quarters, where there is hardly room to stretch your legs, and remaining constantly on the alert, is a tremendous strain on the nerves."

But if there is discomfort below the surface there is peril of death above. Yet a submarine must spend as much time as possible on top of the water, even off the enemy's coast, to spare the precious storage batteries and let the Diesel engines grind oil into electricity by using the electric motor as a dynamo. If she could renew her batteries under water or pick up a useable supply of current as she can pick up a drum of oil from a given spot on the sea-bottom, then the modern submarine would indeed be a hard fish to catch. As it is, great ingenuity has been shown by the German skippers in minimizing the dangers of surface cruising and at the same time stalking their prey. One big submarine masqueraded as a steamer, with dummy masts and funnel. Innocent-looking steam trawlers flying neutral flags acted as screens and lookouts, besides carrying supplies. One of these boldly entered a British harbor, where it was noticed that her decks were cumbered with very many coils of rope. The authorities investigated and found snugly stowed in the center of each a large can of fuel-oil. Another trawler, flying the Dutch flag, was stopped in the

North Sea by a British cruiser and searched by a boarding-party. They were going back into their boat, after finding everything apparently as it should be, when one of the Englishmen noticed a mysterious pipe sticking out of the trawler's side. They swarmed on board again and discovered that the fishing-boat had a complete double hull, the space between being filled with oil. The trawler's crew were removed to the cruiser and a strong detachment of bluejackets left in their place. A few hours afterwards, there was a swirl of water alongside and a German submarine came up for refreshments. It was promptly captured and so was another that presently followed it: a good day's catch for one small fishing-boat.

Because of the uncertainty and danger of depending on underwater caches and tenders, each blockader usually returned at the end of two or three weeks to Heligoland, Zeebruge, Ostend, or some other base to take on supplies, report progress and rest the crew. This of course reduces the number of submarines actually on guard. How large that number may have been at any particular time since the blockade began is unknown to everybody except a few persons in Berlin. At the outbreak of the war, Germany had between twenty and twenty-five submarines in commission and a dozen or so under construction. If, as is claimed, the Germans have been completing a new undersea boat every week since the war began, that would have given them by August 1, 1915, a flotilla of seventy-seven, exclusive of losses. If only thirty had been lost, that would have left fewer than fifty submaines to blockade more than fifty seaports, great and small, scattered over more than twenty-five hundred miles of coast.

Moreover, these widely scattered blockaders would have to be on duty by night as well as by day. But at night or in fog the periscope is useless; to intercept an incoming steamer, running swiftly and without lights, the submarine must rise and cruise on the surface. It cannot use a searchlight to locate the blockade-runner without consuming much precious voltage and at the same time attracting the nearest patrol-boat.

The same disadvantages apply to sending wireless messages from one blockading submarine to another. And as the wireless apparatus of an undersea boat is necessarily low-powered and has a narrow radius, while "oscillators," bells, and other underwater signaling devices are still in their infancy, it would seem as if the German "U-boats" in British waters must have been suffering from lack of coöperation and team-play. If the captain of a Union gunboat, lying off Charleston during the Civil War, caught a glimpse of a blockade runner, he could alarm the rest of the fleet with rockets and signal guns, but the commander of the *U-99* off Queenstown cannot count on his consorts if he himself fails to sink an approaching liner.

Perhaps the most notable shortcoming of the submarine blockade has been its failure to inspire terror. Contrary to the expectations of nearly every forecaster from Robert Fulton to Conan Doyle, the sinking of the first merchant vessels by submarines failed to frighten away any others. Cargo rates are high in war-time and in-

The Submarine Blockade

surance covers the owners' risk, so few sailing orders were canceled. As for the captains, they are not noted for timidity, and professional pride is strong among them; most of them have families to provide for, and every one of them knows that behind him stands an eager young mate with a master's ticket, ready to take the risk and take out the ship if the skipper quits. So the merchant marine accepted the submarine as one of the risks of the trade.

When a big German submarine rose up off the Irish coast within easy gunshot of the homeward-bound British steamer *Anglo-Californian* and signaled for her to heave to, the plucky English skipper slammed his engine-room telegraph over to "Full speed ahead." Away dashed the steamer and after her came the submarine,[2] making good practice with her 8.8 centimeter gun. Twenty shrapnel shells burst over the *Anglo-Californian*, riddling her upper works, slaughtering thirty of her cargo of horses, killing seven of her crew and wounding eight more. Steering with his own hands, Captain Archibald Panlow held his vessel on her course till a shrapnel bullet killed him, when the wheel was taken by his son, the second mate, who brought the *Anglo-Californian* safely into Queenstown. It is men of this breed who have kept Admiral von Tirpitz from saying, in the words of the fictitious Captain John Sirius,

[2] This submarine was the *U-39*. On board her was an American boy, Carl Frank List, who was taken off a Norwegian ship and spent eleven days on the *U-39*, during which time she sank eleven ships. In each case the crew were given ample time to take to the boats. List's intensely interesting narrative appeared in the "New York American" for September 3, 5, and 7, 1915.

"The terror I had caused had cleared the channel."

But because the "Campaign of Frightfulness" has failed and a few score of unsupported submarines have been unable to blockade the British Isles, it is stupid to pretend that there has been no progress since 1901 and say as Admiral von Tirpitz said then,

"Submarines are as useless as ever."

Like every other type of naval craft, submarines are useful but not omnipotent. We have seen what they can do in action and what they have failed to do. As scouts in the enemy's waters they are invaluable. As commerce destroyers, they do the work of the swift-sailing privateers of a century ago. In the fall of 1915, British submarines in the Baltic almost put a stop to the trade between Germany and Sweden. But to blockade a coast effectively, submarines must have tenders, which must have destroyers and light cruisers to defend them, which in turn require the support of battle-cruisers and dreadnoughts, with their attendant host of colliers, hospital ships and air-scouts. Nor can a coast be long defended by submarines, mine-fields and shore-batteries, if there are not enough trained troops to keep the enemy, who can always land at some remote spot, from marching round to the rear of the coast-defenses. This war is simply repeating the old, old lesson that there are no cheap and easy substitutes for a real army and a real navy.

CHAPTER XIV

THE SUBMARINE AND NEUTRALS

BOTH Admiral von Tirpitz and the Austrian Admiralty seem to have begun their submarine campaigns after the method of Captain John Sirius: to starve the enemy any way they could and let the lawyers argue about it afterwards. From the beginning of the blockade, Scandinavian, Dutch, and Spanish vessels, even when bound from one neutral port to another, were torpedoed and sunk without warning by the German submarines. Their governments protested vigorously but without effect. Then came the turn of the United States.

The *Falaba*, a small British passenger steamer outward bound from Liverpool to the west coast of Africa was pursued and overtaken off the coast of Wales on March 28, 1915, by the fast German submarine *U-28*. Realizing that their vessel would be sunk but expecting that their lives would be spared, the crew and passengers began filling and lowering away the boats as rapidly as possible but without panic. The wireless operator had been sending calls for help but ceased when ordered to by the captain of the *U-28*. No patrol boats were in sight and the submarine was standing by on the surface, with both gun and torpedo-tubes trained on the motionless steamer and in absolute command of the situation. Without the slightest excuse or warning, a torpedo was then discharged and exploded against the *Falaba's* side, directly beneath a half-lowered and crowded lifeboat. The lifeboat was blown to pieces and the steamer sunk, with the loss of one hundred and twelve lives, including that of an American citizen, Mr. Leon C. Thrasher, of Hardwick, Massachusetts.

Photo by Brown Bros.
British Submarine, showing one type of disappearing deck-gun now in use.

This cold-blooded slaughter of the helpless horrified the rest of the world and did Germany's cause an incalculable amount of harm. The German people were in no state of mind to realize this, for they had gone literally submarine-mad. They rejoiced in the cartoons depicting John Bull marooned on his island or dragged under and drowned by the swarming " U-boats." They

The Submarine and Neutrals 191

sincerely believed that within a few months the power of the British navy would be broken forever and that in the meanwhile the German submarines could do no wrong. This feeling was presently intensified by the loss of their hero, the gallant von Weddigen. Decorated, together with every man of his crew, with the Iron Cross and promoted to the command of a fine new submarine, the *U-29*, he did effective work as a blockader and captured and sank several prizes, but only after carefully removing those on board. Then the *U-29* was sunk with all hands, by an armed patrol boat, the British declare: treacherously, the German people believe, by a merchant ship whose crew von Weddigen was trying to spare.[1]

No attempt was made to warn the American tank steamer *Gulflight,* bound for Rouen, France, with a contraband cargo of oil, when she was torpedoed by a German submarine on May 1. The vessel stayed afloat but the wireless operator and one of the sailors, terrified by the shock, jumped overboard and were both drowned, while the captain died of heart failure a few hours later on board the British patrol boat that took off the crew and brought the *Gulflight* into port.

On the same day that the *Gulflight* was torpedoed, these two advertisements appeared together in the New York newspapers:

[1] "Von Weddigen, I was told, met his death chasing an armed British steamer. Commanding the *U-29*, he went after a whale of a British freighter in the Irish Sea, signaled her to stop. She stopped but hoisted the Spanish flag. As he came alongside, the steamer let drive with her two four-point-sevens at the submarine, sinking it immediately." Statement of Carl Frank List.

OCEAN STEAMSHIPS.

CUNARD

EUROPE VIA LIVERPOOL
LUSITANIA

Fastest and Largest Steamer now in Atlantic Service Sails
SATURDAY, MAY 1, 10 A. M.

Transylvania,	. . .Fri.,	May 7,	5	P. M.
Orduna,	. . . Tues.,	May 18,	10	A. M.
Tuscania,	. . . Fri.,	May 21,	5	P. M.
LUSITANIA,	. . Sat.,	May 29,	10	A. M.
Transylvania,	. . Fri.,	June 4,	5	P. M.

Gibraltar — Genoa — Naples — Piraeus
S.S. Carpathia, Thur., May 13, Noon.
ROUND THE WORLD TOURS
Through bookings to all principal Ports of the World.
Company's Office, 21-24 State St., N. Y.

NOTICE!

TRAVELERS intending to embark on the Atlantic voyage are reminded that a state of war exists between Germany and her allies and Great Britain and her allies; that the zone of war includes the waters adjacent to the British isles; that, in accordance with formal notice given by the Imperial German Government, vessels flying the flag of Great Britain, or of any of her allies, are liable to destruction in those waters and that travelers sailing in the war zone on ships of Great Britain or her allies do so at their own risk.

IMPERIAL GERMAN EMBASSY,
WASHINGTON, D. C., APRIL 22, 1915.

The Submarine and Neutrals 193

This warning was not taken seriously. It was pointed out that the German submarines had sunk only comparatively small and slow steamers, and generally believed that it would be impossible for them to hit a fast-moving vessel. Not a single passenger canceled his passage on the *Lusitania,* though all admitted that the Germans would have a perfect right to sink her if they could, as she was laden with rifle-cartridges and shell-cases for the Allies. But every passenger knew that he had a perfect right to be taken off first, and trusted to the Government that had given him his passports to maintain it.

The *Lusitania* left New York on the first of May. At two o'clock on the afternoon of Friday, May 7, she was about ten miles from the Irish coast, off the Old Head of Kinsale, and running slowly to avoid reaching Queenstown at an unfavorable turn of the tide, when Captain Turner and many others saw a periscope rise out of the water about half a mile away.

"I saw a torpedo speeding toward us," declared the captain afterwards, "and immediately I tried to change our course, but was unable to manœuver out of the way. There was a terrible impact as the torpedo struck the starboard side of the vessel, and a second torpedo followed almost immediately. This one struck squarely over the boilers.

"I tried to turn the *Lusitania* shoreward, hoping to beach her, but her engines were crippled and it was impossible.

"There has been some criticism because I did not order the lifeboats out sooner, but no matter what may be done there are always some to criticize. Until the *Lusitania* came to a standstill it was absolutely impossible to launch the boats — they would have been swamped."

The great ship heeled over to port so rapidly that by the time she could be brought to a stop it was no longer possible to lower the boats on the starboard side. There was no panic-stricken rush for the boats that could be lowered; all was order and seemliness and quiet heroism. Alfred Vanderbilt stripped off the lifebelt that might have saved him and buckled it about a woman; Lindon Bates, Jr., was last seen trying to save three children. Elbert Hubbard, Charles Klein, Justus Miles Forman, and more than a hundred other Americans died, and died bravely. As the *Lusitania* went down beneath them, Charles Frohman smiled at his companion and said:

"Why fear death? It is the most beautiful adventure of life."

"I turned around to watch the great ship heel over," said a passenger who had dived overboard and swum to a safe distance.

"The monster took a sudden plunge, and I saw a crowd still on her decks, and boats filled with helpless women and children glued to her side. I sickened with horror at the sight.

"There was a thunderous roar, as of the collapse of a great building on fire; then she disappeared, dragging with her hundreds of fellow-creatures into the vortex. Many never rose to the surface, but the sea rapidly grew thick with the figures of struggling men and women and children."

The total number of deaths was more than a thousand.

The most fitting comment on the sinking of the *Lusitania* were the words of Tinkling Cloud, a full-blooded Sioux Indian:

"Now you white men can never call us red men savages again."

Resting its case on "Many sacred principles of justice and humanity," refusing to accept the warning published in the advertising columns of the newspapers by the German embassy either "as an excuse or palliation," and assuming that the commanders of submarines guilty of torpedoing without warning vessels carrying non-combatants had acted "under a misapprehension of orders," the United States concluded its note to Germany, six days after the sinking of the *Lusitania*, with these words of warning:

"The Imperial German government will not expect the government of the United States to omit any word or act necessary to the performance of its sacred duty of maintaining the rights of the United States and its citizens and of safeguarding their free exercise and enjoyment."

Before any reply had been made to this, a German submarine torpedoed without warning the American freight steamer *Nebraskan*, on May 25, a few hours after she had left Liverpool in ballast for the United States. Fortunately no lives were lost, and although the *Nebraskan's* bows had been blown wide open by the explosion, she remained afloat and was brought back to Liverpool under her own steam. The attack was tardily admitted by Germany and explained by the fact that it had been made at dusk, when the commander of the submarine had been unable to recognize the steamer's nationality.

On the last day of May, Germany's answer was received. The Imperial government declared that the *Lusitania* had not been an unarmed merchantman but an auxiliary cruiser of the British navy. That she had had masked guns mounted on her lower deck, that she had Canadian troops among her passengers, and that in violation of American law she had been laden with high explosives which were the real cause of her destruction because they were set off by the detonation of the single torpedo that had been discharged by the submarine.

To these allegations, unaccompanied by the slightest proof and contradicted by the testimony both of British and American eye-witnesses, the United States replied calmly and categorically. It was pointed out that if the German ambassador at Washington or the German consul at New York had complained to the Federal authorities before the *Lusitania* sailed and either guns or troops had been found concealed on her, she would have been interned. The statement of Mr. Dudley Field Malone, collector of the Port of New York, that the *Lusitania* was not armed, may be accepted as final. Gustav Stahl, the German reservist who signed an affidavit that he had seen guns on board her, later pleaded guilty to a charge of perjury and was sentenced to eighteen months in a Federal penitentiary. As for her cargo, every passenger train and steamer in this country is allowed to transport boxes of revolver and rifle cartridges — the only explosives carried on the *Lusitania* — because it is extremely difficult to set off any number of them together, either by heat or concussion.

Dropping these points, Germany then pledged the safety of American ships in the war zone, if distinctly marked, and to facilitate American travel offered to permit the United States to hoist its flag on four belligerent passenger steamers. This, if accepted, would by implication have made Americans fair game anywhere else on the high seas, and was accordingly rejected in the strong American note of July 21.

"The rights of neutrals in time of war," declared President Wilson through the medium of Secretary Lansing, "are based upon principle, not upon expediency, and the principles are immutable. It is the duty and obligation of belligerents to find a way to adapt the new circumstances to them.

"The events of the past two months have clearly indicated that it is possible and practicable to conduct such submarine operations as have characterized the activity of the Imperial German naval commanders within the so-called war-zone in substantial accord with the accepted practices of regulated warfare. The whole world has looked with interest and increasing satisfaction at the demonstration of that possibility by German naval commanders. It is manifestly possible, therefore, to lift the whole practice of submarine attack above the criticism which it has aroused and remove the chief causes of offense."

Repetition by the commanders of German naval vessels of acts contravening neutral rights " must be regarded by the Government of the United States, where they effect American citizens, as deliberately unfriendly."

On July 9, a German submarine discharged a torpedo at the west-bound Cunard liner *Orduna,* narrowly missed her, rose to the surface and fired some twenty shells before the steamer got out of range. Fortunately, none of these took effect. There were American passengers on board and nothing but bad marksmanship averted another *Lusitania* horror.

Three days later, another German submarine stopped an American freight steamer, the *Leelanlaw,* and had her visited and searched by a boarding party, who reported that she was carrying contraband to Great Britain. Because the vessel could not be taken into a German port and there was no time to throw her cargo overboard, the crew were taken off and she was sunk.

Here was a perfectly proper procedure, where no neutral lives had been endangered and the question of the damage to property could be settled amicably in a court of law. It was to the practice in the *Leelanlaw* case that President Wilson referred to so hopefully in his note of July 21. Though the weeks went by without any answer from Germany, it was hoped that the Imperial government had quietly amended the orders to its submarine commanders and that no more passenger ships would be attacked without warning.

But on the 19th of August, the White Star-liner *Arabic* sighted and went to the rescue of a sinking ship. This proved to be the British steamer *Dunsley,* which had been torpedoed by a German submarine. As the *Arabic* came up and prepared to lower her boats, another torpedo from the same submarine exploded against the liner's side, killing several of her crew and sending her to the bottom in eleven minutes. She went down within fifty miles of the resting place of the *Lusitania*. She was sunk without warning and without cause, for she had been bound to New York, with neither arms nor ammunition on board, nor had she made the slightest attempt either to escape or attack the submarine. She carried one hundred and eighty-one passengers, twenty-five of whom were Americans. Two Americans were drowned.

The German government at once asked for time in which to explain, and the Imperial chancellor hinted that the commander of the submarine that sank the *Arabic* might have " gone beyond his instructions, in which case the Imperial government would not hesitate to give such complete satisfaction to the United States as would conform to the friendly relations existing between both governments."

Great was the rejoicing on the first of September, when Ambassador von Bernstorff declared himself authorized to say to the State Department that:

"Liners will not be sunk by our submarines without warning and without safety of the lives of noncombatants, provided that the liners do not try to escape or offer resistance."

But only three days afterwards, the west-bound Canadian liner *Hesperian* was sunk by the explosion of what seemed to have been a torpedo launched without warning from a hostile submarine. And on top of this disturbing incident came the German note on the sinking of the *Arabic,* the perusal of which sent a chill through every peace-lover in America. Affirming that the captain of the *Arabic* had tried to ram the submarine, the note declared that orders had been issued to commanders of German submarines not to sink liners without provocation, but added that if by mistake or otherwise liners were sunk without provocation, Germany would not be responsible.

" The German government," it ran, " is unable to acknowledge any obligation to grant indemnity in the matter, even if the commander should have been mistaken as to the aggressive intention of the *Arabic.*

" If it should prove to be the case that it is impossible for the German and American governments to reach a harmonious opinion on this point, the German government would be prepared to submit the difference of opinion, as being a question of international law, to The Hague Tribunal for arbitration. . . .

" In so doing, it assumes that, as matter of course, the arbitral decision shall not be admitted to have the importance of a general decision on the permissibility . . . under international law of German submarine warfare."

Assuming that this extraordinary stand was based on a misapprehension of the facts, the United States submitted to Germany the testimony of American passengers on the *Arabic,* and the sworn affidavits of her officers, that the submarine had not been sighted from the steamer and that no attempt had been made to ram the undersea boat or do anything but rescue the crew of the *Dunsley.*

By this time a change had come over the spirit of the

Imperial German government. It realized that the submarine blockade of the British Isles had broken down, and that further examples of "Frightfulness" on the high seas would do Germany no good and would probably force the United States into the ranks of Germany's enemies. The sensible and obvious thing to do was to take the easy and honorable way out the American government was holding open. On October 6, Ambassador von Bernstorff gave out the following statement:

"Prompted by the desire to reach a satisfactory agreement with regard to the *Arabic* incident, my government has given me the following instructions:

"The order issued by His Majesty the Emperor to the commanders of the German submarines, of which I notified you on a previous occasion, has been made so stringent that the recurrence of incidents similar to the *Arabic* case is considered out of the question.

"According to the report of Commander Schneider of the submarine which sank the *Arabic,* and his affidavit, as well as those of his men, Commander Schneider was convinced that the *Arabic* intended to ram the submarine.

"On the other hand, the Imperial government does not doubt the good faith of the affidavit of the British officers of the *Arabic,* according to which the *Arabic* did not intend to ram the submarine. The attack of the submarine was undertaken against the instructions issued to the commander. The Imperial government regrets and disavows this act, and has notified Commander Schneider accordingly.

"Under these circumstances, my government is prepared to pay an indemnity for American lives which, to its deep regret, have been lost on the *Arabic*. I am authorized to negotiate with you about the amount of this indemnity."

In the meantime, fragments of the metal box of high explosives that had blown in the side of the *Hesperian* had been picked up on her deck, and forwarded by the British government to America. United States naval experts examined the twisted bits of metal and declared them to have been pieces, not of a mine, as the German government insists, but of an automobile torpedo. However, in view of the fact that the *Hesperian* was armed with a 4.7 gun, and because of the happy outcome of the *Arabic* affair, it seems unlikely that anything will be done about it.

But only a month later there was begun another "Campaign of Frightfulness," this time by Austrian submarines in the Mediterranean. As the passengers on the Italian liner *Ancona*, one day out from Naples to New York, were sitting at luncheon on November 7th, they " felt a tremor through the ship as her engines stopped and reversed."[1] Then, while we were stopping, there was an explosion forward. A shell had struck us.

"When I reached the deck," continues Dr. Greil, "shell was fairly pouring into us from the submarine, which we could see through the fog, about 100 yards away. I hurried below to pack a few things in my trunk. As I was standing over it, a shell came through the porthole and struck my maid, who was standing at my side. It tore away her scalp and part of her skull

---

[1] Statement of Dr. Cecile L. Greil, the only native-born American on board.

and went on through the wall, bursting somewhere inside the ship.

"When I went on deck again I found the wildest excitement. It was like the old-time stories one used to read of shipwrecks at sea. I will not say anything about the crew because I could not say anything good. They launched fifteen boats but only eight got away. I was in one of these. . . . I do not believe the submarine fired deliberately on the lifeboats. They were trying to sink the *Ancona* with shells, but they finally used a torpedo to send her to the bottom. I looked at my watch when she took her last plunge. It was 12.45. We were picked up by the French cruiser *Pluton* about midnight."

The commander of the submarine declared, in his official report, that he had fired only because the *Ancona* had tried to escape, that he had ceased firing as soon as she came to a stop, that the loss of life was due to the incompetence of the panic-stricken crew of the liner, whom the Austrian officer allowed forty-five minutes in which to launch the lifeboats. He admitted, however, that at the expiration of this time he had torpedoed and sunk the *Ancona*, while there were still a number of people on her decks.

About two hundred of the passengers and crew were drowned or killed by shellfire. Among them were several American citizens.

"The conduct of the commander," declared the strongly-worded American note of December 6th, "can only be characterized as wanton slaughter of defenseless non-combatants." . . . The government of the United States is unwilling . . . to credit the Austro-Hungarian government with an intention to permit its submarines to destroy the lives of helpless men, women, and children. It prefers to believe that the commander of the submarine committed this outrage without authority and contrary to the general or special instructions which he had received.

"As the good relations of the two countries must rest upon a common regard for law and humanity, the government of the United States cannot be expected to do otherwise than to denounce the sinking of the *Ancona* as an illegal and indefensible act, and to demand that the officer who perpetrated the deed be punished, and that reparation by the payment of an indemnity be made for the citizens of the United States who were killed or injured by the attack on the vessel."

This undiplomatic language caused no little resentment in Vienna. But after a restatement of the Austrian case, and a much milder rejoinder from Washington, the American demands were apparently acceded to. In the second Austro-Hungarian note, which was published in America on January 1st, 1915, the government of the Dual-Monarchy disavowed the act of its submarine commander, declared that he had acted in violation of his orders and would be punished therefore, and agreed to pay an indemnity for the American citizens who had been killed or injured.

"The Imperial and Royal Government," the note continued, "agrees thoroughly with the American Cabinet that the sacred commandments of humanity must be observed also in war. . . . The Imperial and Royal Government can also substantially concur in the principle expressed ... that private ships, in so far as they do not attempt to escape or offer resistance, may not be destroyed without the persons aboard being brought into safety."

Like the settlement of the *Arabic* case, this was hailed as a great diplomatic victory for the United States. Unlike it, there was no question of sharing the credit with the anti-submarine activities of the Allies, whose merchant ships in the Mediterranean were being torpedoed with startling frequency. On December 21st, the new 12,000 ton Japanese liner *Yasaka Maru* was sunk without warning, near Port Said. Thanks to the splendid discipline of her crew, no lives were lost. There was an alleged American on board, but there was some irregularity about his citizenship papers. Nor were there any Americans aboard the French passenger ship *Ville de la Ciotat,* torpedoed on Christmas Eve, with the loss of seventy lives. There was nothing to mar the smug satisfaction of the American people on New Year's Day.

Then came the news of the sinking of the Peninsular and Oriental liner *Persia,* on December 30th, off the Island of Crete.

"I was in the dining room of the *Persia* at 1.05 P.M.," declares Mr. Charles Grant of Boston, who was one of the two Americans on board. "I had just finished my soup, and the steward was asking me what I would take for my second course, when a terrific explosion occurred.

"The saloon became filled with smoke, broken glass and steam from the boiler, which appeared to have burst. There was no panic on board. We went on deck as though we were at drill, and reported at the lifeboats on the starboard side, as the vessel had listed to port. . . .

"The last I saw of the *Persia*, she had her bow in the air, five minutes after the explosion. . . .

"Robert McNeely, American Consul at Aden, sat at the same table with me on the voyage. He was not seen, probably because his cabin was on the port side.

"It was a horrible scene. The water was black as ink. Some passengers were screaming, others were calling out good-by. Those in one boat sang hymns."

The *Persia* was apparently torpedoed, without warning. Like the *Hesperian*, she was armed with a 4.7 gun. One of the ship's officers saw the white wake of the torpedo. But no one saw the submarine.

The commander of that submarine evidently believed, like Captain Sirius, in striking first and letting the lawyers talk about it afterwards.

INDEX

A-1, 124.
A-3, 124, 135.
A-5, 125.
A-7, 124.
A-8, 124, 126.
Aboukir, 160, 169.
Accidents, 124.
Aeroplanes, 17, 71, 172.
Air-chamber, 47.
Alabama, 70.
Albemarle, 43, 166.
Alert, 136.
Alkmaar, 4.
Alstitt's submarine, 75.
Ancona, 202.
Anglo-Californian, 187.
Apostoloff's submarine, 66.
Arabic, 198, 205.
Argo, 92.
Argonaut, 85, 92, 98.
Argonaut, Jr., 85.
Argus, 34.
Asia, 12.
Aube, Admiral, 59.
Audacious, 161, 169.
Awash condition, 127.

B-2, 124.
B-11, 165.
Badger, 168.
Baker's submarine, 82.
Balance-chamber, 44, 48.
Ballast-tanks, 16, 38, 57, 82, 111, 138.
Baralong case, 164, note.
Barber, Lieutenant F. M., 16.
Barlow, Joel, 26, 34.
Bates, Jr., Lindon, 194.
"Battle of the Kegs," 23.
Bauer, Wilhelm, 56, 65, 120, note.
Beatty, Admiral, 175.
Beauregard, General, 39.

Belridge, 148.
Berwick Castle, 124.
Bigskorth, Squadron Commander, 172.
Birmingham, 159.
Blake, Mr., 10.
Blockade, 177 *et seq.*
"Blowing the tanks," 63, 112, 122, 128.
Booms, 92, 171.
Borelli, 10.
Boucher's submarine, 66.
Bourgois, Captain, 57.
Bourne, William, 4.
Boush, Rear Admiral, 137.
Bouvet, 154.
Boyle, Robert, 7.
British Hollands, 80.
British Navy, 30, 70, 72, 175, 178.
Brun, Monsieur, 57.
Bulwark, 161.
Buoyancy chamber, 49.
Bushnell, David, 6, 13 to 25, 28, 95, 128, 154.

C-11, 124.
C-14, 124.
Cable-cutting, 89, 95.
Cairo, 144.
Caldwell, Lieutenant H. C., 78, 79.
Caprivi, 148.
Carlson, Captain, 40.
Cerberus, 22.
Chandler, Mr. Edward F., 53.
Chlorin gas, 126, 129, 137.
Clairmont, 34, 81.
Commodore Jones, 144.
Compass, 18, 113.
Compensation-tank, 79, 118.
Compressed-air tank, 30, 57, 131.
Conning-tower, 12, 15, 28, 78, 103, 113.

207

Index

Constantin's submarine, 66.
Cooking, 108.
Copper sheathing, 18, 35.
Cressy, 160, 169.
Crilley, Frank, 137.
Cushing, Lieutenant, 43, 166.

D-5, 155.
Daniels, Secretary, 81, 138.
Dardanelles, the, 64, 147, 154, 165.
David, 36, 43, 61.
Davis, Commander, 52.
Day, J., 10, 128.
Delaying-valve, 47.
Demologos, 35.
Depth-control, 113.
Destroyers, 35, 104, 168, 170.
Delfin, 124.
Dewey, Admiral, 79, 145.
Diable Marin, 65, 120, note.
Diesel, Dr., 108.
Diesel engines, 104, 135, 184.
Divers, 14, 40, 56, 136.
Diving-bells, 4.
Diving compartment, 83, 88, 94, 130, 132.
Diving-planes, 28, 38, 48, 71, 72, 78, 111.
Dixon, Lieutenant, 40.
Dorothea, 32.
Doughty, Thomas, 115.
Doyle, Sir Arthur Conan, 178, 186.
Drzewiecki, 64, 71.
Dunsely, 198.
Dubilier, Mr. W., 171.

E-4, 160.
E-5, 124.
E-9, 156.
E-11, 165.
E-13, 164.
E-15, 165.
Eagle, 12, 18.
Edison battery, 126.
Eel-boats, 4, 14.
Electric Boat Company, 81, 96.
Electric motors, 108, 184.
Electric submarines, 59, 60, 66, 83, note.

Emerald Isle, 72.
Emergency drop-keel, 10, 15, 83, 128.
Enver Pasha, 166.
Ericsson, John, 82, 104.
Escape from sunken submarine, 130.
Even-keel submergence, 61, 96.

F-4, 124, 136.
Falaba, 189.
Faotomu, Lieutenant Takuma, 128.
Farfadet, 124.
Farragut, Admiral, 142.
Fenian Brotherhood, 71.
Fenian Ram, 73.
Fessenden oscillator, 119, 125.
Fishing for submarines, 170, 183.
Foca, 124.
Folger, Commander, 82.
Forman, Justus Miles, 194.
Formidable, 162, 169.
Frohman, Charles, 194.
Fulton, 135.
Fulton, Robert, 26 to 35, 69, 139, 186.

Gages, 20, 112, 129.
Garett, Rev. Mr., 61.
Gasoline engines, 86, 105.
Gasoline fumes, 90, 107, 125.
German contributions, 107, 115.
Gimlets, 16, 18, 64.
Goubet submarines, 60.
Grant, Charles, 205.
Greased leather, 6, 9.
Greil, Dr. Cecile L., 202.
Giuseppe Garibaldi, 169.
Gulflight, 191.
Guns, 83, 102, 174, 187, 202.
Guncotton, 46.
Gustave Zédé, 59.
Gymnote, 59.
Gyroscope, 50, 53, 114.
Gyroscopic compass, 113.

Hague Tribunal, 148, 200.
Halstead, 56.

Index

Hammond, Jr., Mr. John Hays, 55.
Hanson, Captain, 183.
Harsdoffer, 5, 6.
Hatsuse, 147.
Hautefeullie, Abbé de, 7.
Hela, 155.
Hermes, 161, 168.
Hesperian, 199, 202, 206.
Hogue, 160, 169.
Holbrook, Commander, 165.
Holland, John P., 68 to 81, 95, 104, 115, 175.
Holland, 76 to 81, 86, 103, 104, 125.
Holland No. 1, 70.
Holland No. 2, 71.
Holland No. 8, 76.
Holland Torpedo-boat Company, 75, 79, 81.
"Horn of the Nautilus," 29.
Housatonic, 40.
Howard, Ensign, 36.
Hovgaard, Commander, 75.
Huascar, 50.
Hubbard, Elbert, 194.
Hundley, 38 to 41.
Hydroplanes, 84, 95.
Hydrostatic valve, 48, 128, 154.

Intelligent Whale, 56, 81, 86.
International law, 178, 179, 200.
Irresistible, 154, 161.

James I, 5.
"Jammer," the, 46.
Jefferson, Thomas, 14, 16, 22, 25.
Jonson, Ben, 3, 64.

K-class, 138.
Kambala, 124.
Kearsarge, 78.
Kheyr-el-din, 165.
Klein, Charles, 194.
Krupps, the, 99.

Labeuf, Monsieur, 91.
Lacavalerier, Señor, 66.
Lacomme, Dr., 64.
Lake, Mr. Simon, 82 to 99, 175.

Laurenti, Major Cesare, 134.
Laurenti dock, 124.
Le Son, 9.
Lee, Ezra, 15 to 22.
Leelanlaw, 198.
Leon Gambetta, 169.
Leveling-vanes, 96.
Lifeboats, 131.
List, Carl Frank, 187, 191.
Lord St. Vincent, Admiral, 32.
Lupuis, Captain, 44.
Lusitania, 181, 192 to 198.
Lutin, 124.

McNeely, Robert, 206.
Maine, 76.
Majestic, 166.
Makaroff, Admiral, 147.
Malone, Mr. Dudley Field, 196.
Marblehead, 146.
Maryland, 137.
Merrimac, 69.
Mersenne, 6, 91.
Messudieh, 165.
Microphones, 171.
Mines, Confederate, 143, 154, note.
  contact, 139, 144, 148 to 155, 179.
  drifting, 23, 139, 154.
  electric, 89, 144, 151.
  observation, 144.
Mine-field, 151, 165.
Mine-planter, 146, 149.
Mine-sweeping, 139, 152.
Moltke, 164.
Monitor, 42, 69, 81.
Mother-ship, 100, 111, 135.
Mute, 35.

Napier, John, 4.
Napoleon, 27, 32, 33.
Narval, 91.
Nautilus, Fulton's, 27 to 31, 56, 72.
Nautilus, Jules Verne's, 59.
Navigating bridge, 103, 111.
Nebraskan, 195.
Nemo, Captain, 59.
New Ironsides, 36, 144.

Index

New York, 78.
Nordenfeldt, 28, 61, 74, 95.
Nordenfeldt II, 62, 78, 83.
Notes, American, 180, 195 to 197, 200, 203.
  Austrian, 204.
  British, 181.
  German, 191, 199.
No. 6, 124, 128.

Oars, 6, 9, 16, 17, 66.
Ocean, 154.
Oil-engine, 60, 78, 104.
Olympic, 162, 178.
Orduna, 198.
Osage, 115.
Oxygen, 7, 131.
Ozark, 100.

Panlow, Captain Archibald, 187.
Panoramas, 26.
Payne, Lieutenant, 39.
Pendulum, 49, 53.
Peral, 64, 66.
"Peripatetic Coffin," 39.
Persia, 205.
Persius, Captain, 183.
Periscope, 78, 83, 114, 125, 186.
Petropavlosk, 147.
Philip, Captain, 146.
Phosphorescence, 6, 19.
Pipe-masts, 86, 95.
Pitt, 32.
Plongeur, 57, 132.
Plunger, 75.
Pluton, 203.
Pluviôse, 124, 125, 134.
Pneumatic gun, 79.
Pommern, 163.
"Porpoise dive," 78, 160.
Porter, Admiral David, 40.
"Primer," the, 46.
Propellers, adjustable, 82.
  primitive, 16, 28.
  transverse, 83.
  vertical-acting, 16, 28, 61, 83, 95, 154.
Protector, 95.
Pumps, 16, 28, 111.

Ramillies, 35.
Ramming, 124, 168, 200.
Reducing-valve, 48.
Rescuing, 125, 156.
Resurgam, 61.
Riou, Olivier, 59.
Rogers, Commodore, 34.
Rotterdam Boat, 9, 14, 69.
Royal Edward, 166.
Rudders, bow, 96, 111.
  horizontal (see diving-planes).

S-126, 169.
San Francisco, 149.
Safety-buoy, 132.
  catch, 47.
  helmets, 130.
  jackets, 130.
Sails, 29, 31.
Salvage docks, 134.
Sampson, Admiral, 89, 146.
Schneider, Commander, 201.
Scope, Lieutenant Perry, 100.
Searchlight, 86, 186.
Selfridge, Rear-admiral, 115.
Servo-motor, 49, 53.
Sirius, Captain John, 177, 187, 189, 206.
Skerrett, Mr. R. G., 135.
Spuyten Duyvil, 42.
Stahl, Gustav, 196.
"Staple of News, the," 3.
Steam submarine, 61.
Steamboat, 32, 34.
Storage-batteries, 59, 126, 184.
"Striker," the, 46.
Stromboli, 42.
Submarine fighting submarine, 174.
Submarine railroad, 64.
Submersible, 91.
Superstructure, 90, 102.
Symons's submarine, 9.

Taylor, D. W., Chief Constructor, U. S. N., 96.
Telephoning from submarines, 88, 132.
Tecumseh, 142.
Templo, Alvary, 71.

Index

Texas, 146.
Thrasher, Leon C., 190.
Tinkling Cloud, 195.
Tissot, Professor, 171.
Torpedo, automobile, 44 to 55.
  boats, 45, 103.
  Brennan, 59.
  Chandler, 53.
  controllable, 43, 54, 55.
  cost of, 47, 103.
  Davis gun-, 52.
  Fulton's anchored, 139.
  Hammond wireless, 55.
Torpedo-nets, 34, 170.
  origin of name, 29.
  practice, 116.
  recovering, 47, 123.
  Schwartzkopf, 52, 160.
  Sims-Edison, 54.
  spar, 37, 43.
  tubes, 45, 46, 63, 117, 118, 133, 138.
  wake of, 49, 206.
"Torpedo War and Submarine Explosions," 35, 139.
Torpedo, Whitehead, 44 to 52, 117.
Transports, 166, 171, 178.
Trim, 96.
Trimming-tanks, 117.
Trinitrotuluol, 52.
Triumph, 166.
Trumbull, Governor, 14.
Turner, Captain, 193.
Turtle, 12, 14 to 22.

U-1, 108.
U-3, 124, 132.
U-9, 160.
U-12, 169.
U-15, 159.
U-16, 183.
U-28, 189.
U-29, 191.
U-39, 187, note.
U-51, 166.

Vanderbilt, Alfred, 194.
Vand der Wonde, Cornelius, 6.
Van Drebel, Cornelius, 4 to 9, 41.
Vendémiaire, 124.
Vereshchagin, 147.
Vickers Sons & Maxim, 80.
Ville de la Ciotat, 205.
Von Weddigen, Lieutenant-commander, 18, 160, 191.
Von Bernstorff, Ambassador, 199.
Von Tirpitz, Admiral, 69, 177, 187, 189.
Vulcan, 132.

Waddington, Mr. J. F., 83, note.
War-head, 47, 52.
War Zone, 30, 179.
Washington, George, 13, 17, 25.
Wheeled submarines, 84.
White mice, 13, 110.
Whitehead, Mr., 44.
Whitney, Secretary, 74.
Wilson, President, 180, 197, 198.
Wright brothers, 71.

X-4, 102 to 123.

Yasaka Maru, 205.
Yenisei, 146.

Zeppelins, 172.

www.ingramcontent.com/pod-product-compliance
Lightning Source LLC
Chambersburg PA
CBHW021705230426
43668CB00008B/736